LITTLE GREY RABBIT'S PATTERN BOOK

Pamela Peake

based on characters created by
ALISON UTTLEY
and
MARGARET TEMPEST

COLLINS

William Collins Sons & Co Ltd
London · Glasgow · Sydney · Auckland
Toronto · Johannesburg

The coloured illustrations to accompany the instructions were drawn by Tracey Williamson

Photographs on pages 9, 23, 31, 41, 51 and on the front cover by Graham Miller

Photographs on pages 8, 24, 32, 42, 50 by Geoff Goode

Designed by Enid Fairhead

This book is published in co-operation with the Alison Uttley Literary Property Trust

British Library Cataloguing in Publication Data

Peake, Pamela
Little Grey Rabbit's pattern book:
based on the characters created by
Alison Uttley and Margaret Tempest.
1. Soft toy making – Juvenile literature
I. Title
745.592′4 TT174.3
ISBN 0-00-194205-0

Printed and bound in Spain by Cronion S.A., Barcelona

Introduction

LITTLE GREY RABBIT
page 8

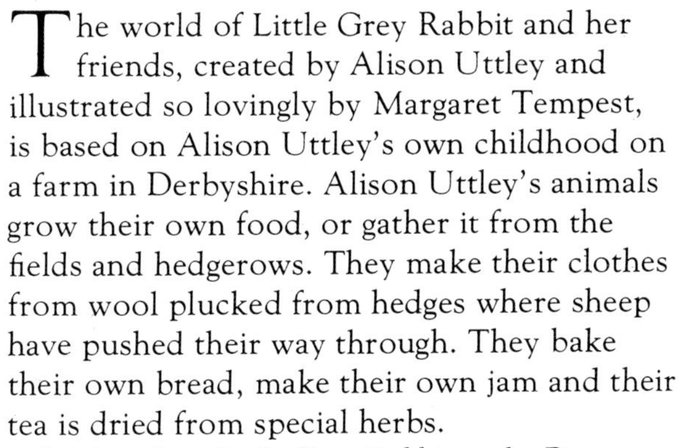

The world of Little Grey Rabbit and her friends, created by Alison Uttley and illustrated so lovingly by Margaret Tempest, is based on Alison Uttley's own childhood on a farm in Derbyshire. Alison Uttley's animals grow their own food, or gather it from the fields and hedgerows. They make their clothes from wool plucked from hedges where sheep have pushed their way through. They bake their own bread, make their own jam and their tea is dried from special herbs.

In the play, *Little Grey Rabbit to the Rescue*, Milkman Hedgehog warns Little Grey Rabbit that a Weasel has come to live in a cottage nearby. One day, the Weasel captures Squirrel and Hare and plans to cook them for his dinner. But Little Grey Rabbit creeps into the Weasel's house and bravely rescues them.

Pamela Peake has taken the five characters from the play and designed patterns and clothes for each of them. All the patterns are printed exact size on the page and when made up the animals are about 30cm high. The clear instructions are easy to follow, and great care has been taken to ensure that the finished toys are perfect replicas of the animals established by Margaret Tempest for Alison Uttley's stories.

OLD HEDGEHOG
page 31

SQUIRREL
page 23

HARE
page 52

WEASEL
page 41

General directions

Patterns
All the patterns for the animals and their clothes are printed full size except for some simple pieces like skirts which are given as measurements. Use tracing paper to make a copy of each pattern piece. Mark in position of match points, eyes, darts, openings and make a note of cutting instructions. (Cut a pair means cut a Left and Right. Cut 2 means cut two the same.) Just a few of the patterns are too large to fit on the page so only half is shown. Trace these patterns onto folded doubled paper with the fold matching the fold of the pattern. Cut tracings out and glue them onto a card backing. Card patterns can be used as templates for drawing round and thereby remove the need to use pins.

Buying fabrics
All the fabrics and accessories needed to make and dress each character are given in the materials list. Select the fur fabrics carefully with regard to depth of pile and colour. There are many wonderful simulated animal skins to choose from and you should have little difficulty in finding the quality needed. Fabrics for the clothes should be lightweight so that they drape well and are not too bulky when gathered. They should also be washable so that they can be kept clean.

Layouts
Fabric allowance has been calculated with patterns placed across the full width of the fabric. Always position large pieces first then fit the smaller

pieces into the remaining area for an economical layout. The arrows on the patterns indicate the straight grain of fabric (with clothes fabrics, the grain lies parallel to the selvage). When using fur fabric, it is important to remember the direction in which the pile lies. Generally the pile should stroke back from the nose and down the body towards the tail and up to the top of the ears. Place fur fabric pile side down on the cutting surface and mark round pattern pieces with a soft pencil. The arrows on the patterns must lie in the same direction as the stroke of the pile.

Cutting

Check carefully before cutting out that you have the correct number of pieces and that when instructed to cut a pair you have remembered to turn the pattern over so that you cut a Left and a Right. Slide the lower point of the scissors between the pile of fur fabrics, cutting the backing only. Never try to cut a double thickness of fur. Before removing pattern from fabric, transfer all necessary markings. Mark match points and eye positions by making a hole in the pattern and then marking through with a soft pencil.

Seams

All seams are 6mm ($\frac{1}{4}$in) from the cutting edge unless otherwise stated. A little extra has been allowed for gathers and hems.

Stitching

The animals have been stitched by hand. However before starting it will be necessary to trim the fur pile in the seam allowance as short as possible to reduce the bulk. Tack pieces right side together to prevent slipping. Seams are worked in backstitch with a strong thread. Any fur trapped in the seam allowance may be picked out with a needle by gently stroking the seam on the right side. Finger press all seams open.

The clothes can be stitched by machine or by hand using a tiny neat running stitch. The edges of gathered seams will need to be trimmed to reduce the bulk.

Filling

Use a good quality white synthetic toy filling such as polyester. This is hygenic, lightweight and has good bounce which means that it springs back to shape after crushing – features that will contribute to the success of your characters. Remove small amounts of filling from the bag and tease apart to fluff up the fibres. Insert in toy skin and build up the shape, using your hands to mould the body from the outside.

How to fix safety eyes
Patterns are marked with the position for fixing eyes. However if you use different furs to those specified in the materials list or even sew outside the seam allowance you will need to determine a new position for the eyes. This is quickly and easily done by filling the head with stuffing then placing an eye on the surface and moving it about until happy with the appearance. Press the shank of the eye firmly against the fur to leave an impression. Pierce this position with an awl and then feed the shank of the eye into the head and fix washer over shank with the prongs facing away from the eye. Press washer firmly downwards until it is locked tightly against the back of the eye with the fur sandwiched between.

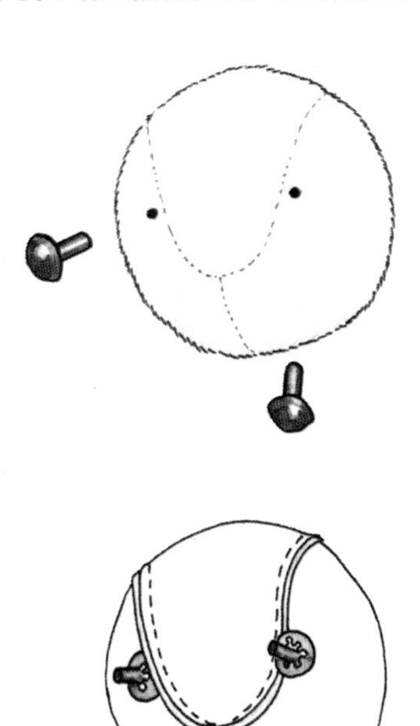

Eyes fixed in this way meet the safety requirements of the Toys (Safety) Regulations 1974 and will not provide a danger for children under normal conditions of play. Embroidered eyes are an alternative if you are at all worried about using commercial toy components.

Ladder stitch
This is an invaluable stitch for toymakers. It is used to close all openings along seam lines that have been left open for turning skins right side out and stuffing. It is also used to attach ears to heads, heads to bodies, tails to bodies and fixing limbs in a set position.

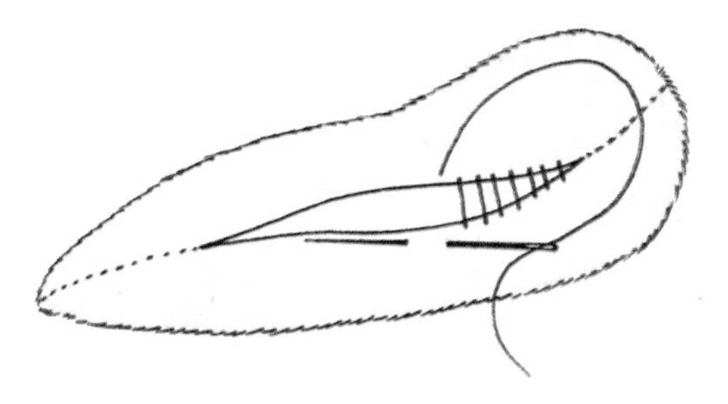

Thread a long needle with doubled nylon. Take a small stitch in the cheek, leaving a length of nylon free on the outside to make the first two whiskers. Work several tiny backstitches to anchor the thread, tugging to make sure. Now leave a long loop and work more tiny backstitches to anchor the loop. Pass needle through to the other side of the head, anchor with backstitches, work a loop, anchor again and then cut the threads some distance away. Cut both loops and trim whiskers to required length.

Whiskers

A set of whiskers makes a very attractive finish, greatly adding to the charm of the characters. Invisible nylon sewing thread has been used to make these whiskers and they have all been worked in the same way but cut to different lengths.

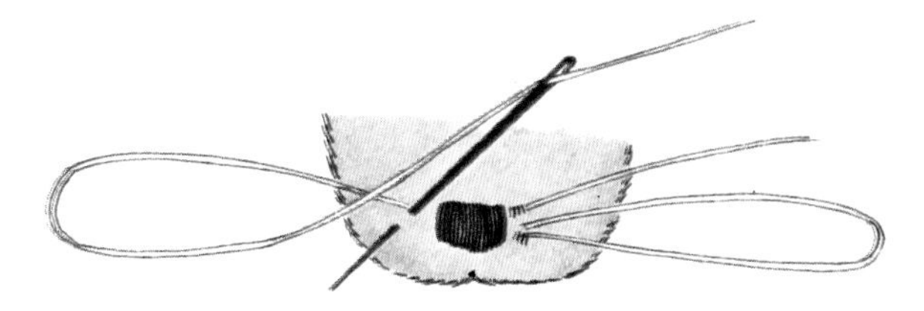

Work ladder stitch from right to left along the seam line with a strong doubled thread in your needle. Pull up tightly on thread and the stitches should be invisible while the raw edges of the seams will automatically turn inwards. When sewing a head to a body you will find it easier if you use a long darning needle and work around the head several times getting the stitches really close by working between stitches of the previous round.

How to make a tape hinge

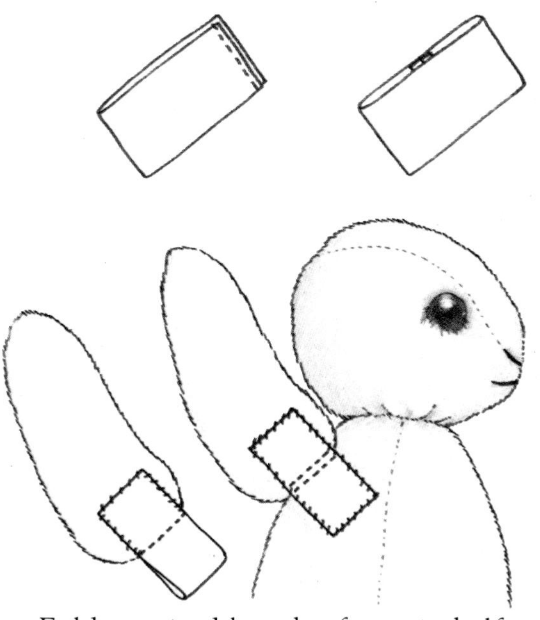

Fold required length of tape in half and stitch the ends together. Turn seam inwards and position centrally. Sew half of the doubled tape to the inside top of the arm with buttonhole stitch along the outside edges and then across the top with a small backstitch. Now place arm against correct side of body and sew the free end of the tape hinge securely in place.

Materials

For the body – height 29cm (11½in)

1. Grey beaver quality fur with a pile depth of 12/13mm (½in)
   23cm of 137cm wide fabric (¾yd × 54in)
2. Grey velour or velveteen for soles
   15cm (6in) square
3. Short pile white fur for ear linings
   15cm (6in) square
4. White fur for tail with a pile depth of 25mm (1in)
   15cm (6in) square
5. Embroidery thread for nose
6. Grey tape 22cm (9in) long, 25mm (1in) wide

For the clothes

7. White cotton for petticoat, collar and cuffs
   30.5cm of 114cm (⅓yd × 45in) wide fabric
8. Grey cotton for dress
   30.5cm of 114cm (⅓yd × 45in) wide fabric
9. Blue cotton for apron
   23cm of 114cm (¼yd × 45in) wide fabric
10. Broderie anglais to trim petticoat
    51cm (20in) long, 22mm (⅞in) wide

Also:
150g (6oz) stuffing
A pair of 15mm brown safety eyes
Nylon thread for whiskers
4 × 6mm press studs for petticoat
2 × 7mm press studs for dress

Little Grey Rabbit

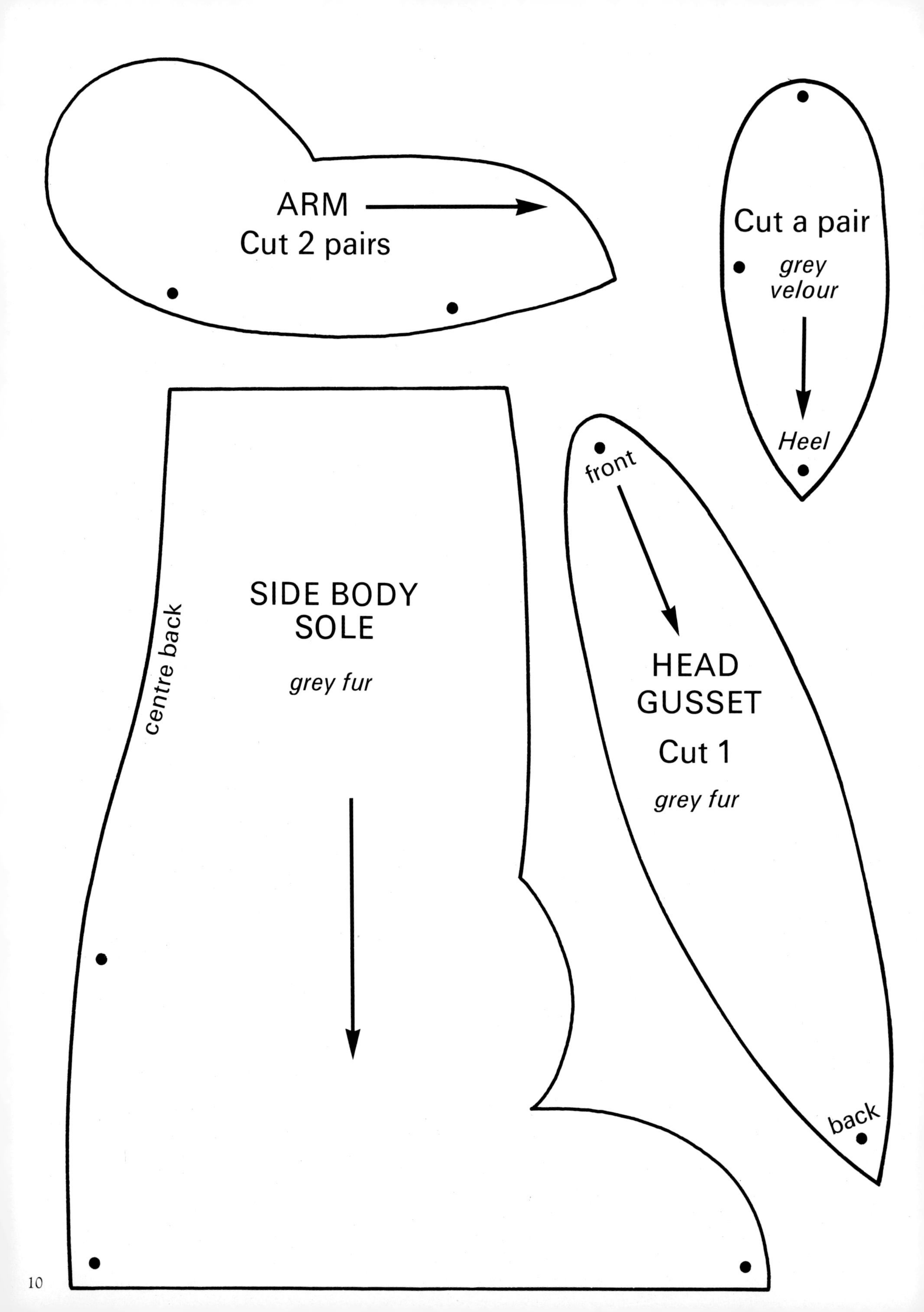
ARM
Cut 2 pairs
Cut a pair
grey
velour
Heel
front
HEAD
GUSSET
Cut 1
grey fur
back
SIDE BODY
SOLE
grey fur
centre back

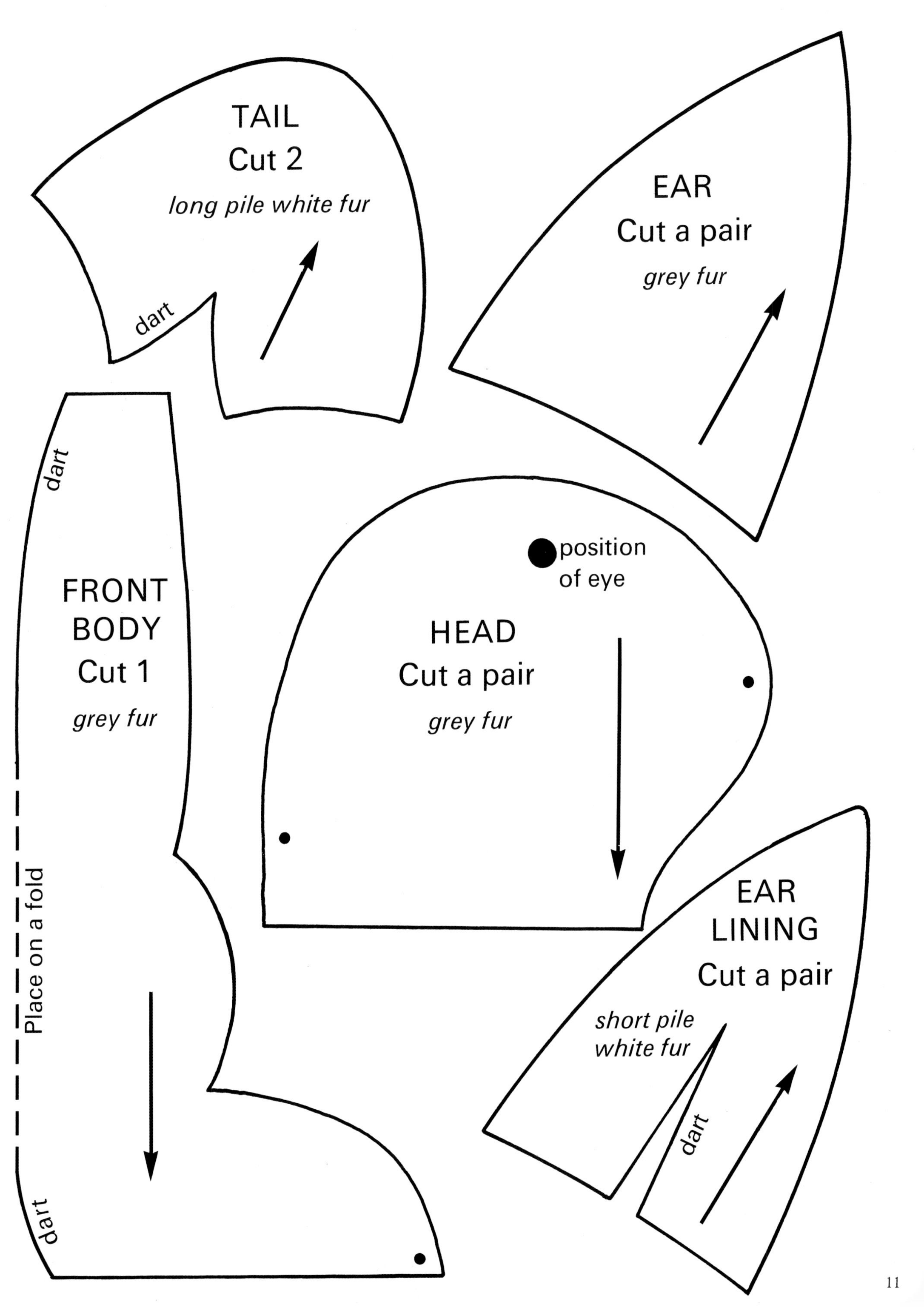
TAIL
Cut 2
long pile white fur
dart
EAR
Cut a pair
grey fur
FRONT
BODY
Cut 1
grey fur
dart
Place on a fold
dart
position
of eye
HEAD
Cut a pair
grey fur
EAR
LINING
Cut a pair
short pile
white fur
dart

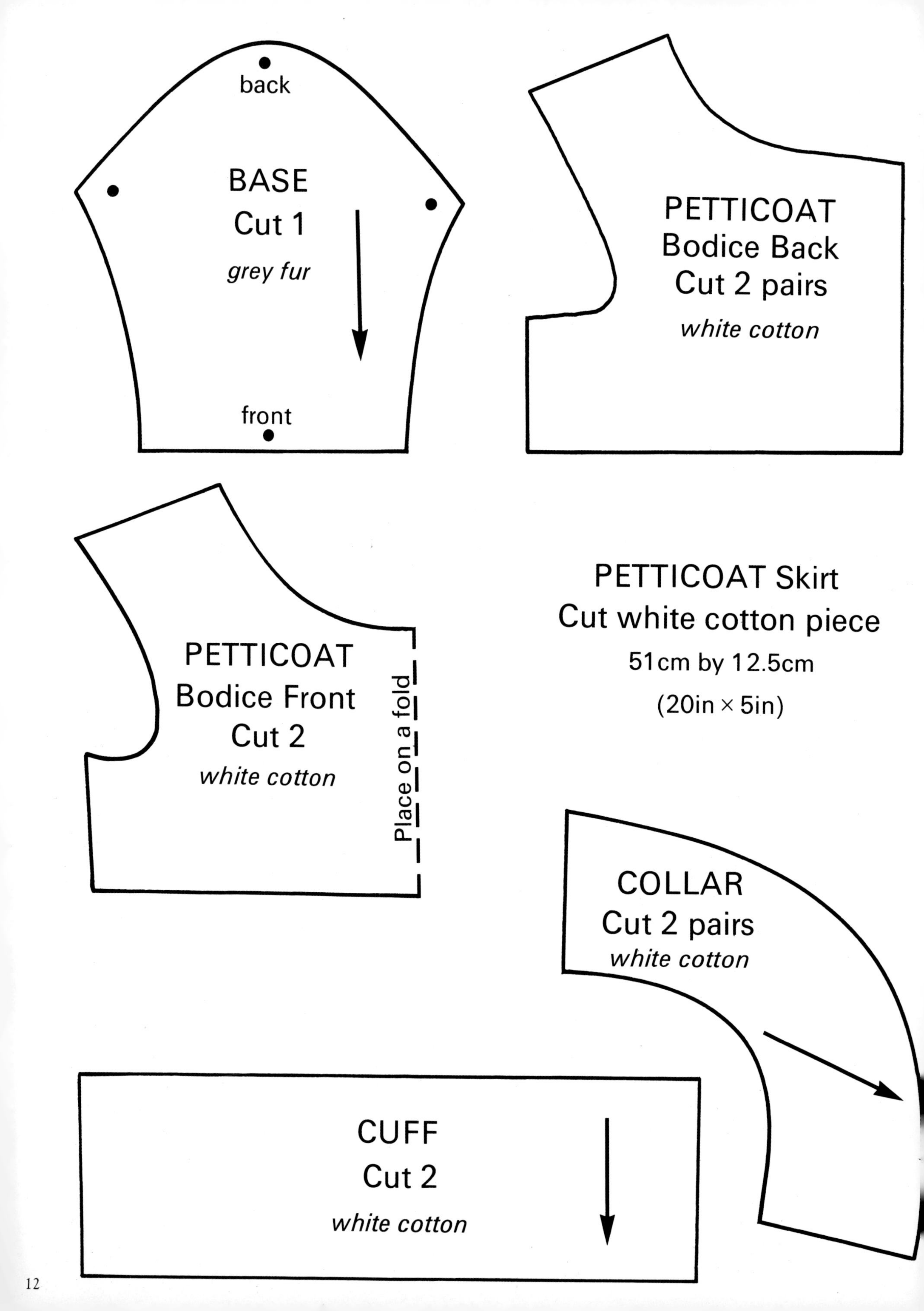
back
BASE
Cut 1
grey fur
front
PETTICOAT
Bodice Back
Cut 2 pairs
white cotton
PETTICOAT
Bodice Front
Cut 2
white cotton
Place on a fold
PETTICOAT Skirt
Cut white cotton piece
51cm by 12.5cm
(20in × 5in)
COLLAR
Cut 2 pairs
white cotton
CUFF
Cut 2
white cotton

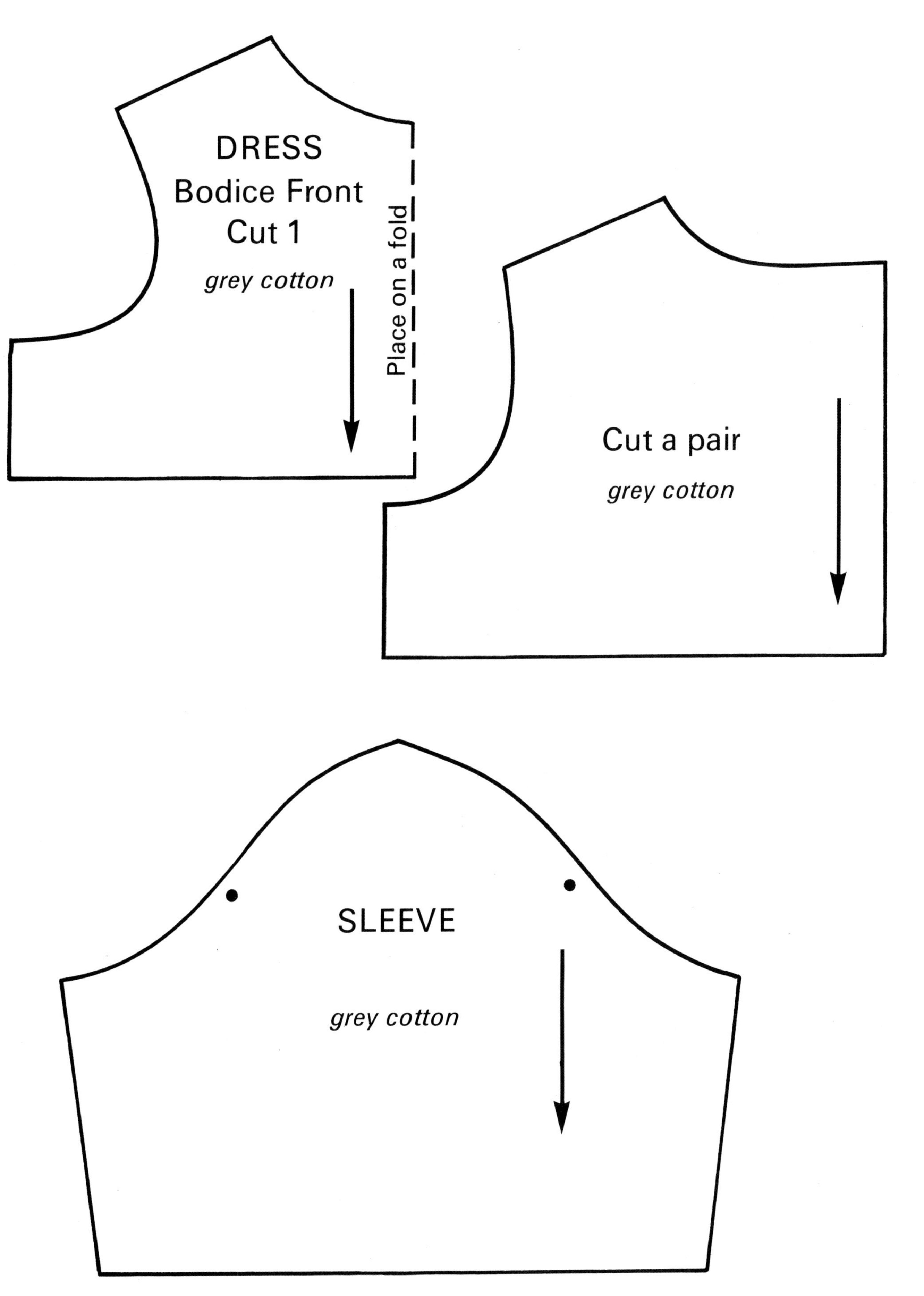
DRESS
Bodice Front
Cut 1
grey cotton
Place on a fold
Cut a pair
grey cotton
SLEEVE
grey cotton

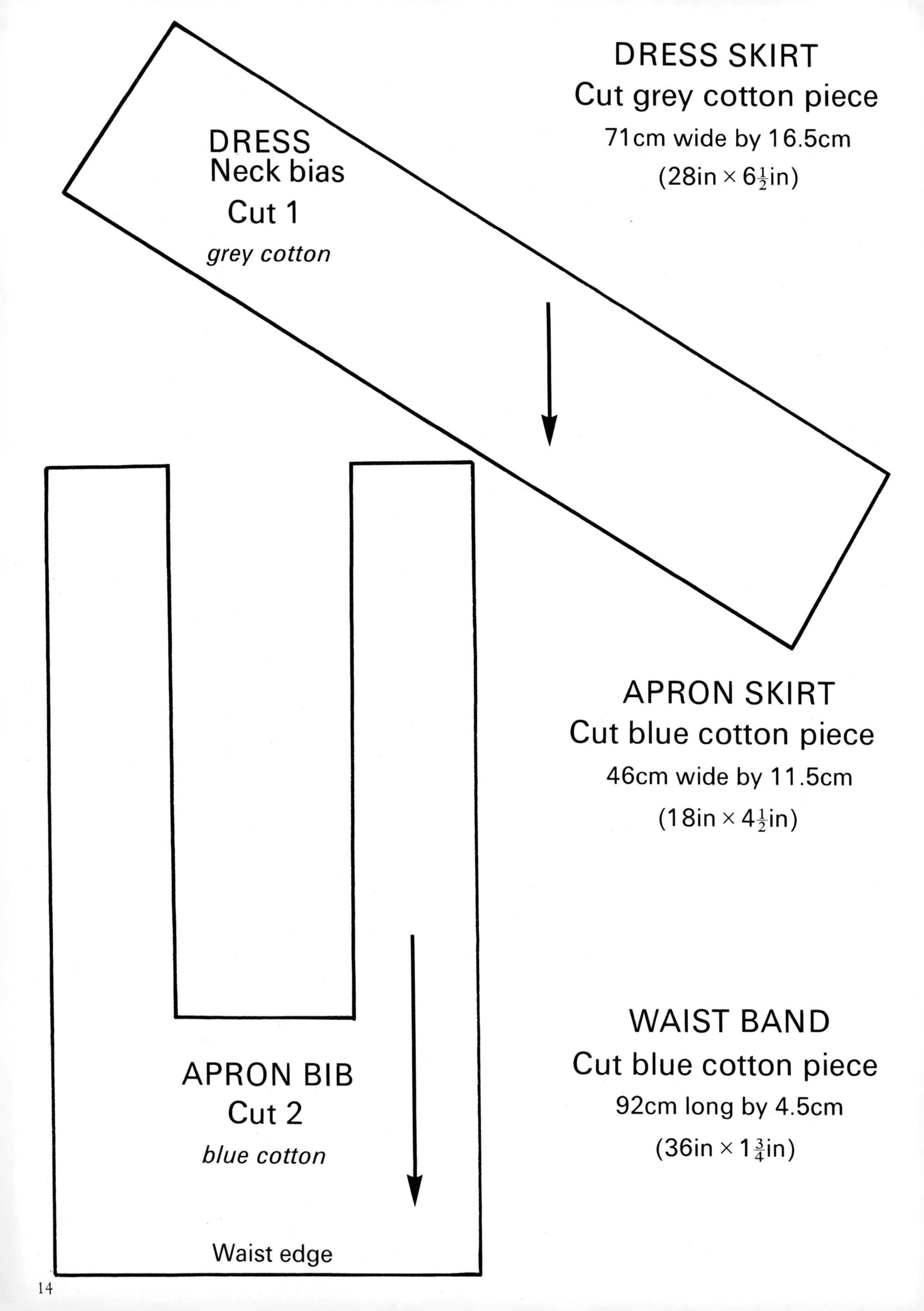
DRESS SKIRT
Cut grey cotton piece
71cm wide by 16.5cm
(28in × 6½in)
DRESS
Neck bias
Cut 1
grey cotton
APRON SKIRT
Cut blue cotton piece
46cm wide by 11.5cm
(18in × 4½in)
WAIST BAND
Cut blue cotton piece
92cm long by 4.5cm
(36in × 1¾in)
APRON BIB
Cut 2
blue cotton
Waist edge

Making the body

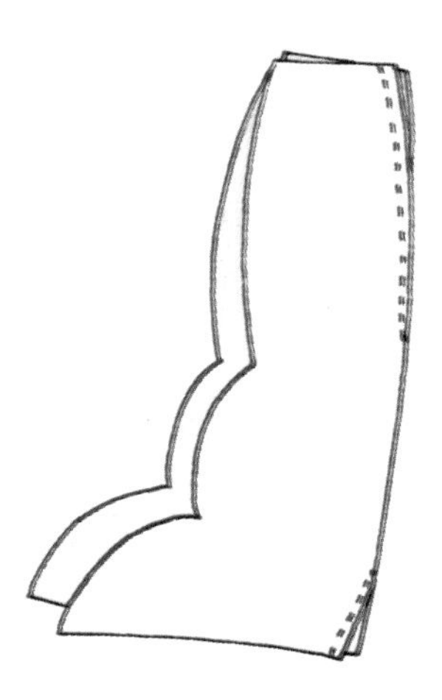

1 Fold the front body in half lengthways and sew the two darts.

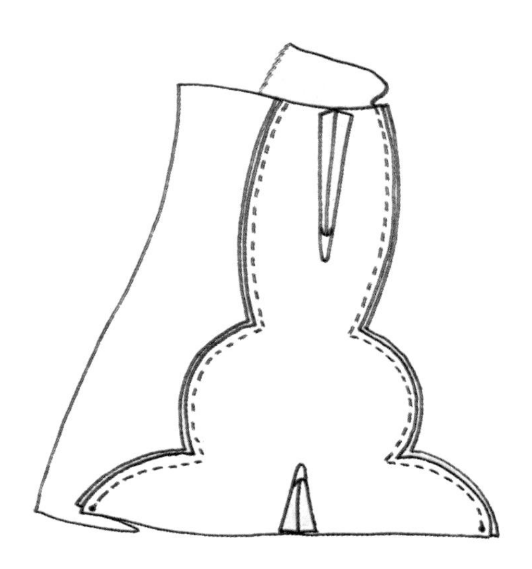

2 Sew each side body in turn to the front body starting at the neck edge and working down to the feet.

3 Bring side bodies together and sew the centre back seam from the match point to the lower edge.

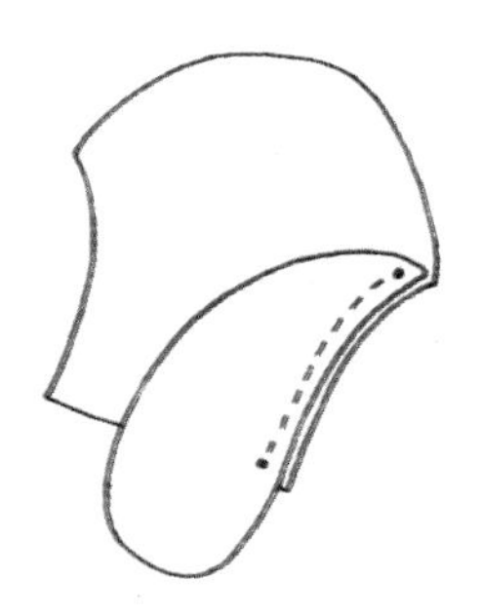

4 Sew sole to base along inside edge starting from match point at heel. Take care not to stretch the curve. Sew second sole to other side of the base in the same way.

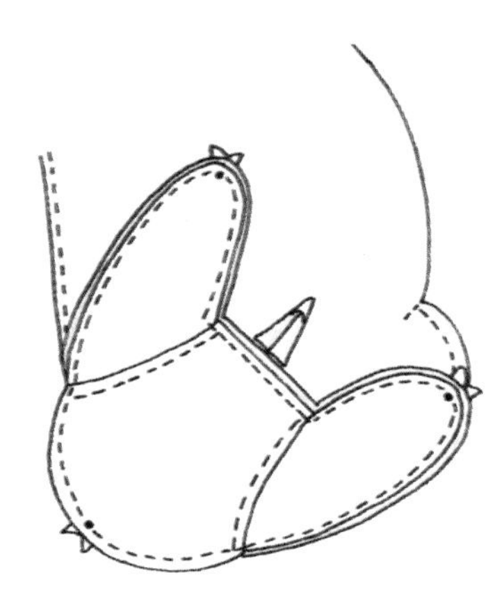

5 Fit completed base into bottom of body. Match points line up against centre back, centre front and toe seams. Sew in place with all seams opened flat.

6 Finish sewing remainder of centre back seam up to neck edge.

7 Turn completed skin right side out and check all seams before stuffing. Fill feet firmly and mould haunches by hand as you continue filling up to the neck. Shave fur away from base. This will enable the Rabbit to sit without rocking.

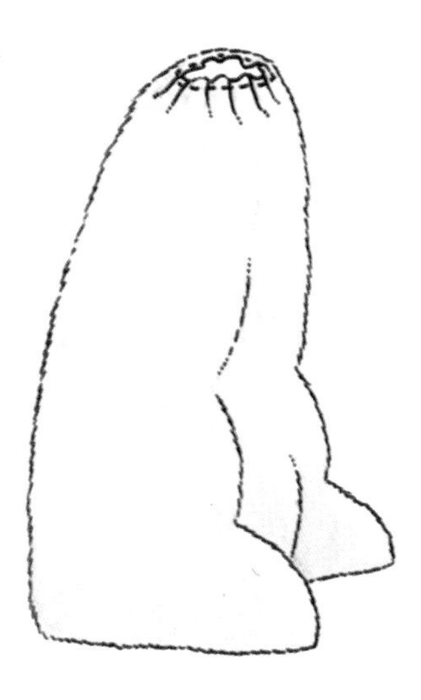

8 Run a strong doubled gathering thread around the neck, pull up, drawing edges inwards and together. Fasten off securely.

9 Make the tail by sewing the dart in each piece then sew them together leaving the lower edge open. Turn right side out and lightly stuff. Close opening by oversewing the raw edges together.

10 Ladder stitch the tail to the body.

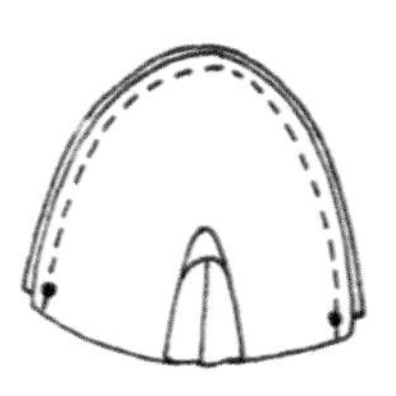

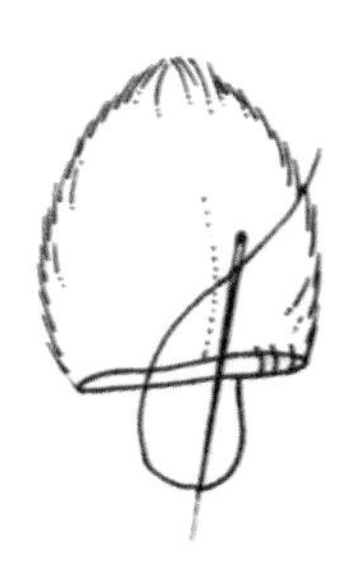

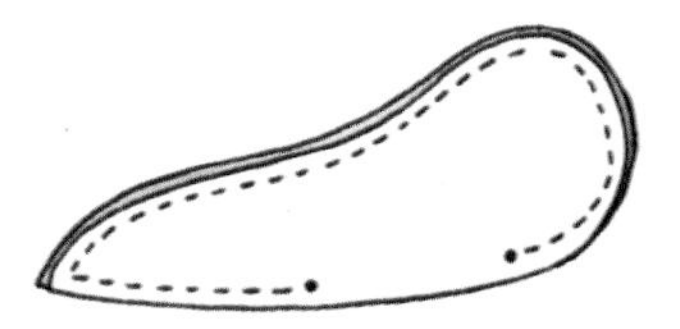

11 Sew a pair of arm pieces together and turn right side out. Stuff lightly and close opening with ladder stitch. Make a tape hinge using an 11cm ($4\frac{1}{2}$in) length. Sew to arm then sew arm to the body. Make remaining arm in the same way.

12 Sew head pieces together from match point at nose down to neck edge.

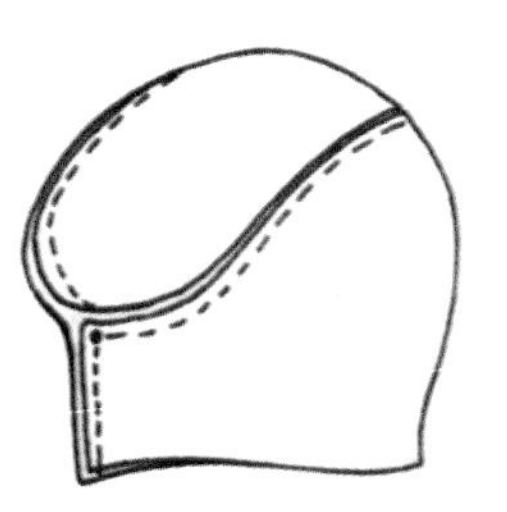

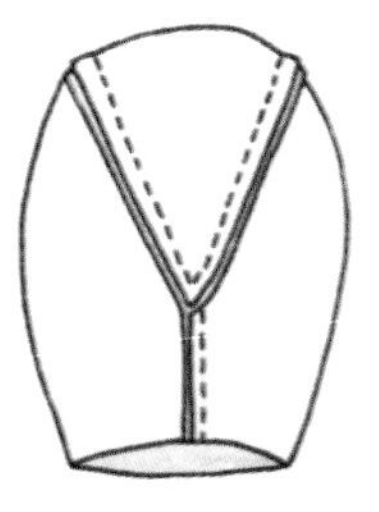

13 Fit gusset between head pieces making sure that the rounded end is placed to the front. Sew each side in turn from front to back. Close short centre back seam of head beyond gusset down to neck edge.

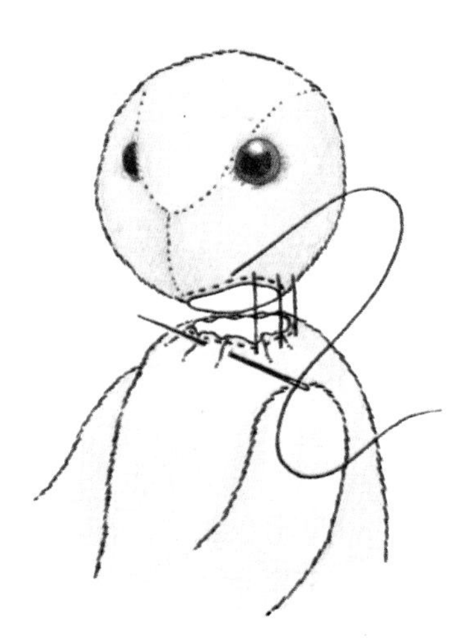

14 Turn head right side out and fix eyes in place. Stuff head firmly, rounding out the cheeks. Run a strong doubled gathering thread around the neck edge and pull up firmly. Fasten off. Ladder stitch head to body.

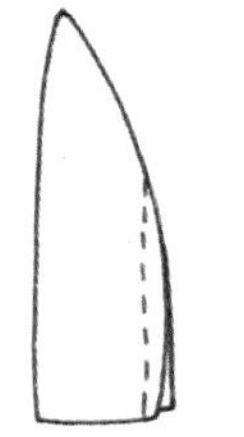 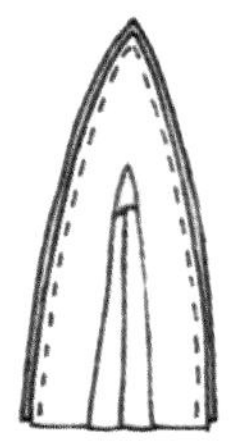 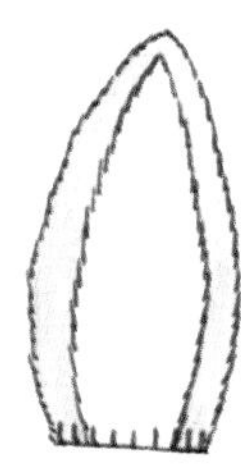

15 Make darts on the ear linings then sew each lining to a grey ear piece. Turn right side out and oversew bottom raw edges together.

Fold each corner of the ears inwards so that the grey frames the linings. Stitch in place then ladder the front first then across the back.

16 Embroider nose and mouth using all six strands of embroidery thread. (The stitches lie on the gusset and nose seam.)

17 Sew a few whiskers to the cheeks and trim to required length.

18 Groom the body by brushing and releasing any fur that might be trapped in the seams. Trim fur around eyes to make a more pleasing appearance.

Now make Little Grey Rabbit's clothes

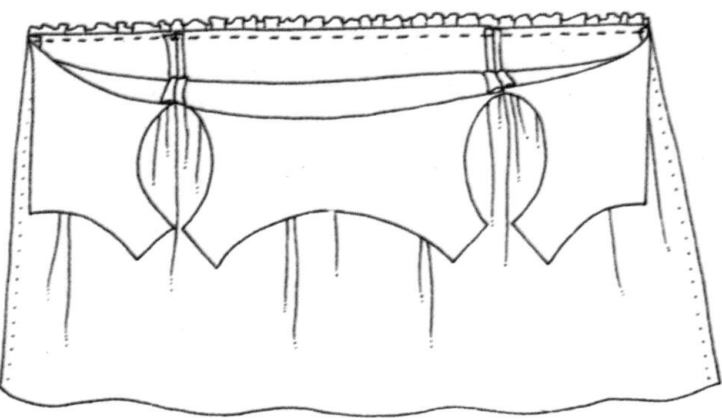

3 Make a narrow hem on each short back edge of the petticoat skirt. Gather a long edge and pull up to fit the waist. Match skirt top to bodice bottom, keeping the lining pulled back out of the way. Spread the gathers evenly and sew.

THE PETTICOAT

1 Match bodice backs to bodice front and sew underarm side seams. Press seams open. Prepare lining in the same way.

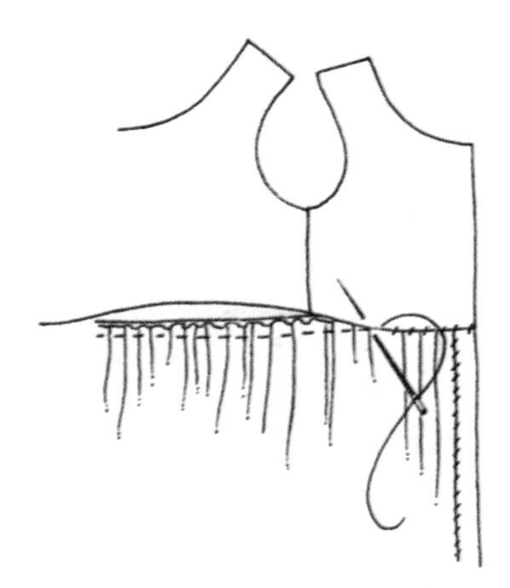

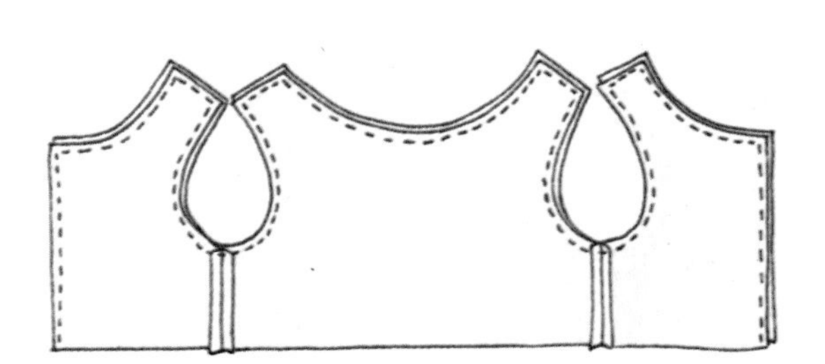

2 Lay bodice and lining right sides together and sew a continuous seam from the back waist edge round the neck and armholes to the opposite side. Trim away seam edges to reduce bulk and clip the curves to release tension. Turn right side out and press.

4 Press seam towards bodice. Turn under waist edge of lining and hem in place.

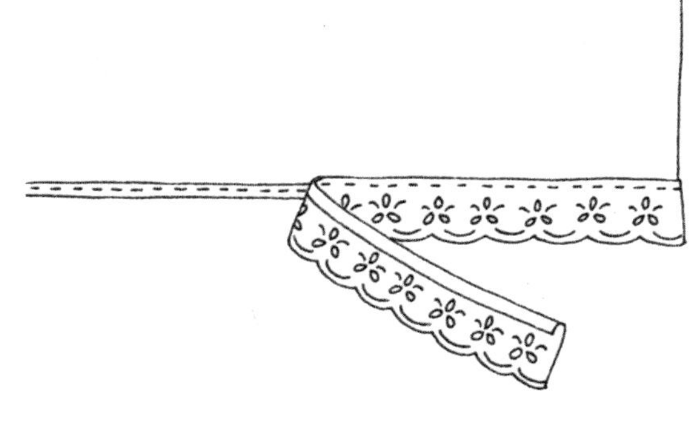

5 Turn bottom edge of petticoat onto right side, press and stitch. Press under raw edge of broderie anglais and stitch in place over the raw edge of the turning. Finish petticoat by sewing tiny press studs on shoulders and back opening of the bodice.

THE DRESS

1 Sew bodice backs to bodice front at shoulders. Press seams open.

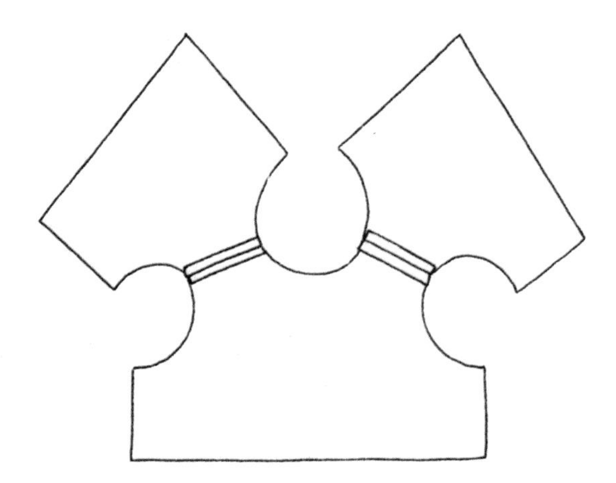

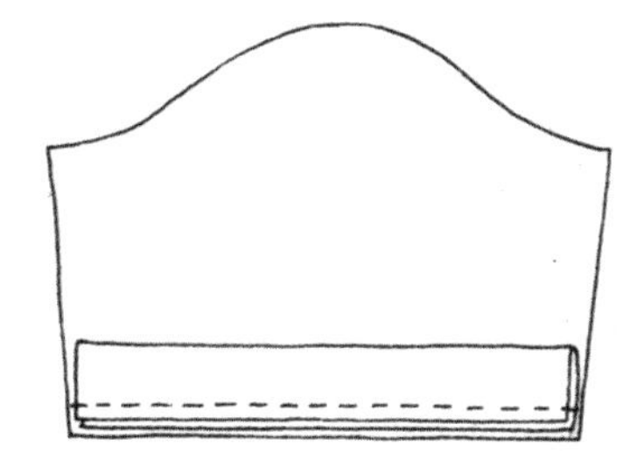

2 Fold cuff in half across the width with wrong sides together. Press. Sew to wrong side of sleeve with all raw wrist edges level.

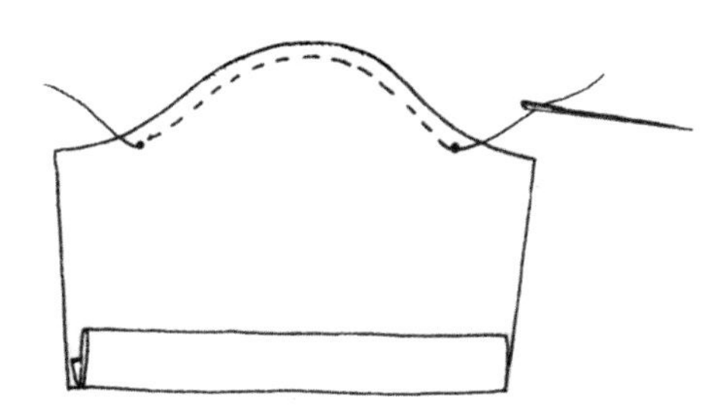

3 Turn cuff to right side of sleeve and press upwards. Gather between match points at head of sleeve.

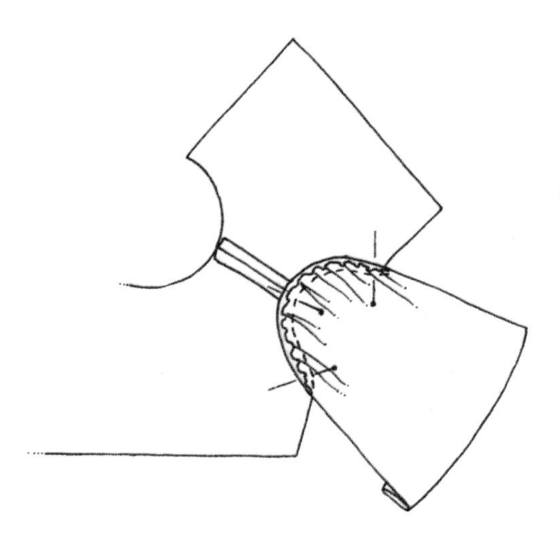

4 Fit sleeve into armhole. Pin at each side and shoulder. Pull up gathers to fit. Sew. Trim seam close to stitching and clip to release tension. Make second sleeve and sew to bodice in the same way.

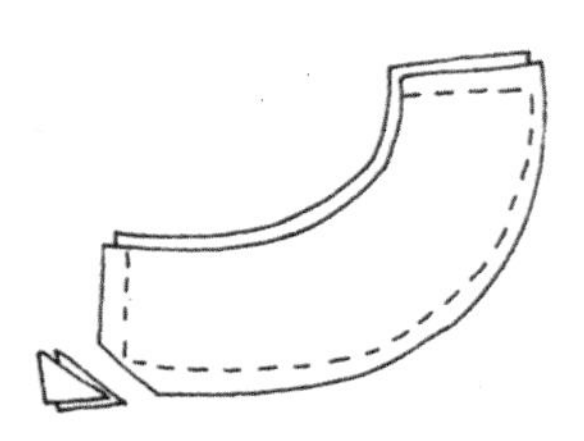

Take care not to catch any folds of the bodice into the curved seam. Trim seam close to stitching line then clip so that the neck can be stretched out straight.

5 Sew two collar pieces together round outside edge. Trim seam and clip corners off. Make other collar in the same way.

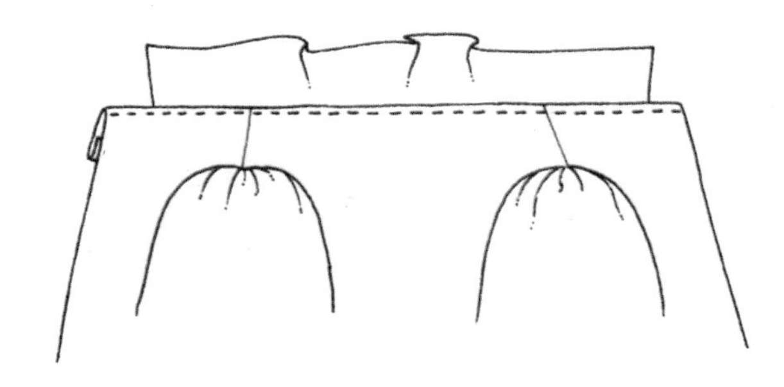

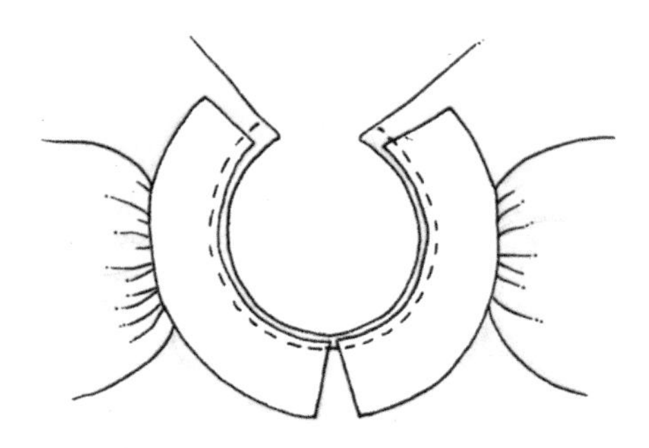

8 Turn bias strip over to wrong side of bodice and collar upwards, away from the bodice. Stitch bodice and bias together close to the neck edge.

6 Turn collars right side out and press. Position on right side of bodice with front edges touching and sew. Check that the neck opening fits your Grey Rabbit and make any adjustments at this stage.

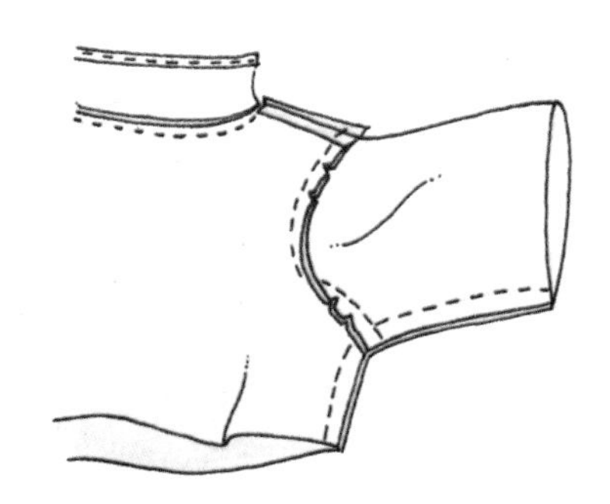

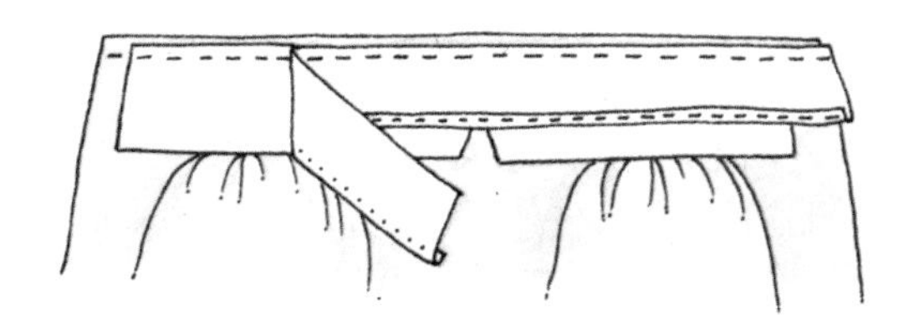

9 Fold bodice on each side in turn to match underarm and bodice sides. Sew and turn right side out.

7 Turn under and neaten one long edge of the neck bias. Lay opposite long raw edge of this strip over collar at neck edge and sew.

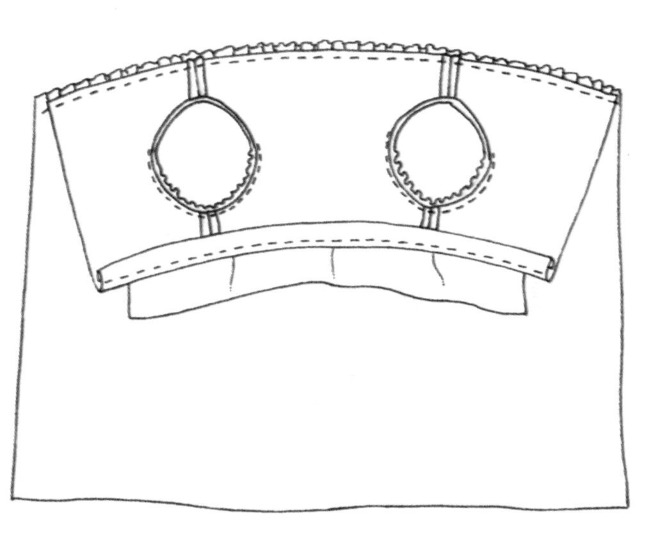

10 Gather one long edge of dress skirt then match it to the bodice with right sides facing and raw edges level. Pull up gathers spreading the fullness evenly. Sew. Trim the seam and press towards the bodice.

12 Make a narrow hem down each back edge of the dress and fit on Little Grey Rabbit before hemming bottom edge. Turn up a deeper hem along the bottom edge. This can be stitched behind the tuck. Sew press studs at neck and waist to fasten dress at back.

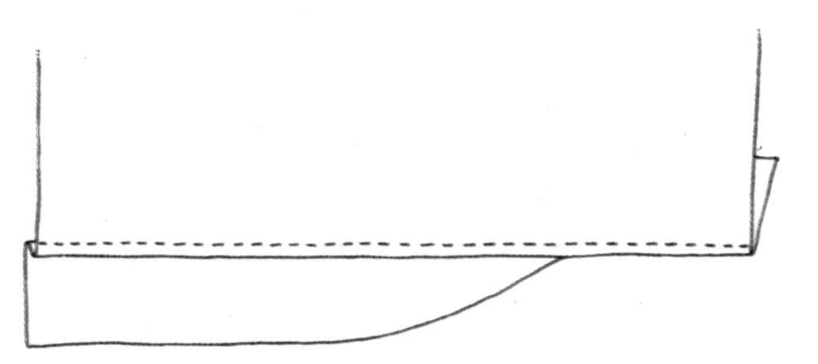

11 Make a narrow tuck along the bottom of the skirt by folding up 4.3cm ($1\frac{3}{4}$in) to the wrong side and sewing close to the edge. Open out the fold and press the tuck downwards.

THE APRON

1 Sew both apron bibs together leaving ends of strap and waist edge open. Trim seams and clip at front corners. Turn right side out and press.

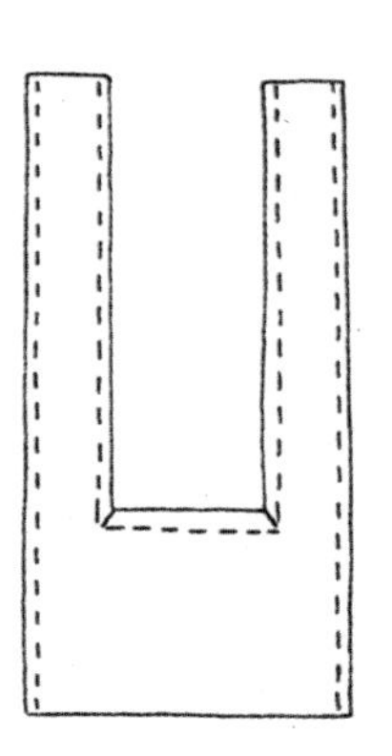

2 Make a narrow hem on both short sides of apron skirt. Gather one long edge to form the waist. Pull gathers up to 20.5cm (8in). Lay apron bib centrally against gathers with raw edges level and right sides together. Sew in place.

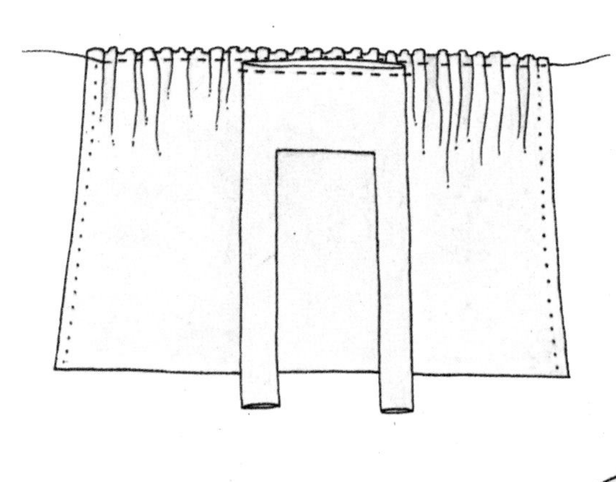

3 Sew waist band to gathered edge of skirt. Fold end of band right sides together and sew from the end towards the skirt. Sew other end of waist band in the same way.

4 Turn both ends of the waist band right side out and press. Fold under seam allowance of open edges, press, slip stitch edges together and across the back of the apron skirt.

5 Sew ends of shoulder straps to back edge of apron. Dress Little Grey Rabbit in her clothes and measure required length of apron. Hem lower edge.

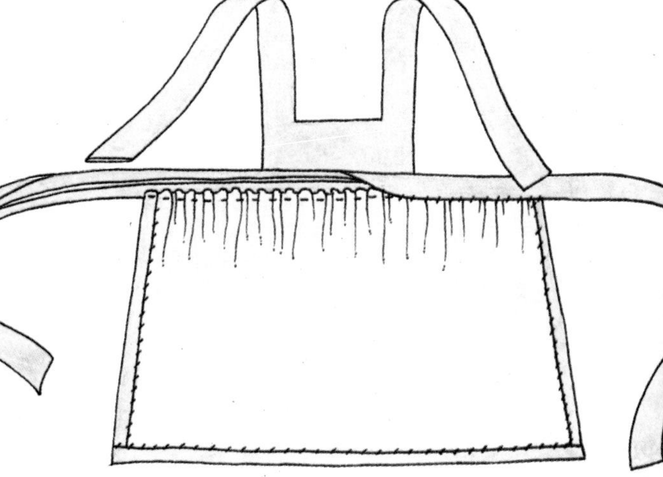

Squirrel

Materials

For the body – height 28cm (11in)

1. Short pile unpolished rust fur for body
   23cm of 137cm wide fabric ($\frac{1}{4}$yd × 54in)
2. Long pile rust fur for tail with a pile depth of 25mm (1in)
   30.5cm (12in) square
3. Long pile brown fur for ears with a pile depth of 25mm (1in)
   23cm (9in) square
4. Beige velour or velveteen for soles
   15cm (6in) square
5. Dark brown embroidery thread for nose
6. Brown tape 22cm (9in) long, 25mm (1in) wide

For the clothes

7. White cotton for petticoat
   30.5cm of 114cm wide fabric ($\frac{1}{3}$yd × 45in)
8. Pink cotton for dress
   30.5cm of 114cm wide fabric ($\frac{1}{3}$yd × 45in)
9. Broderie anglais to trim petticoat
   51cm (20in) long by 22mm ($\frac{7}{8}$in) wide
10. Dark brown Setaskrib fabric marker pen
11. Pale yellow ribbon
    92cm (1yd) long by 25mm (1in) wide
12. Dark brown velvet ribbon
    30.5cm (12in) long by 10mm ($\frac{3}{8}$in) wide

Also:
150g (6oz) stuffing
Pair of 15mm brown safety eyes
4 × 6mm press studs for petticoat
2 × 7mm press studs for dress
Small black hook for belt

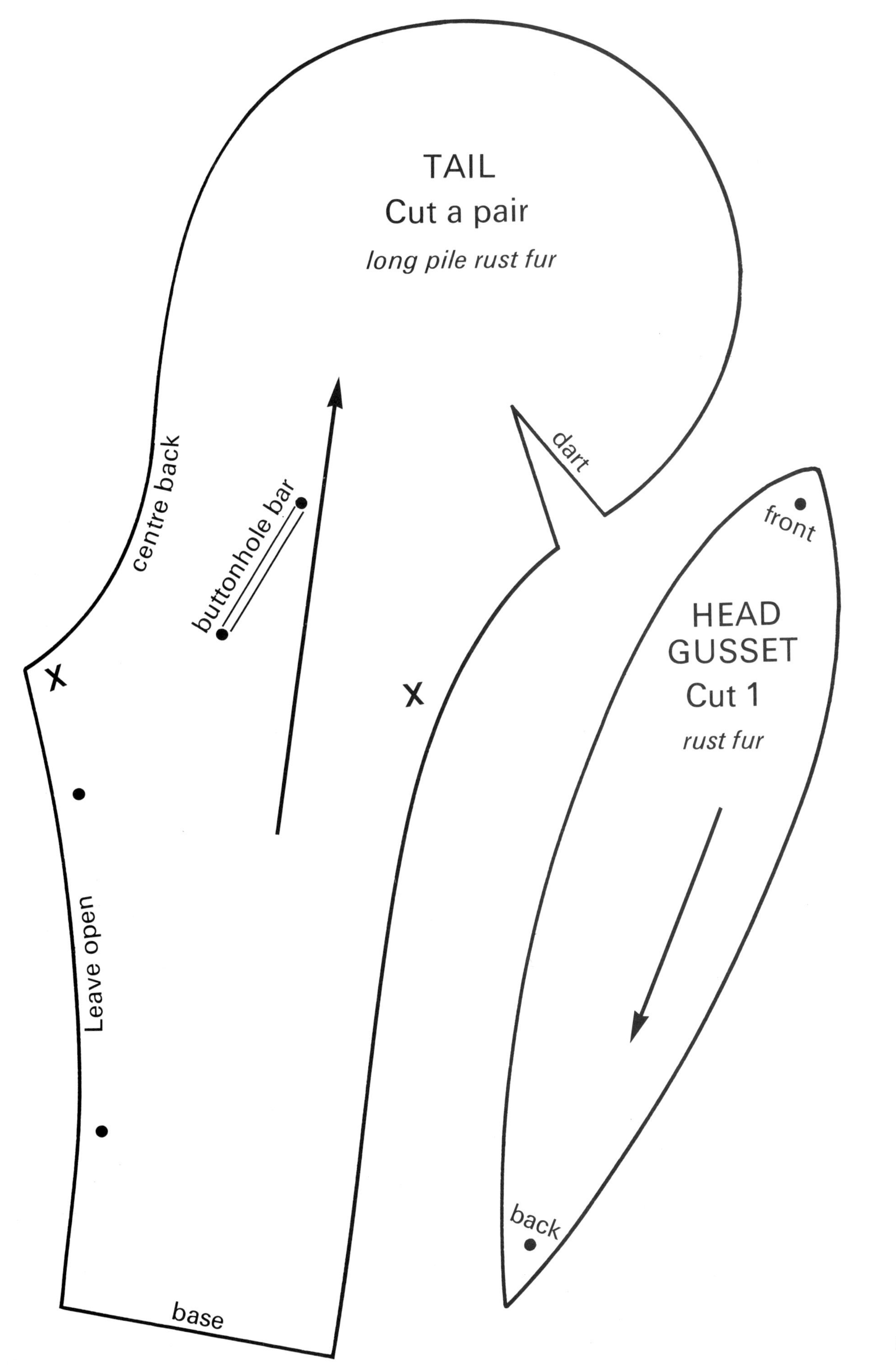
TAIL
Cut a pair
long pile rust fur
dart
centre back
buttonhole bar
X
X
Leave open
base
front
HEAD
GUSSET
Cut 1
rust fur
back

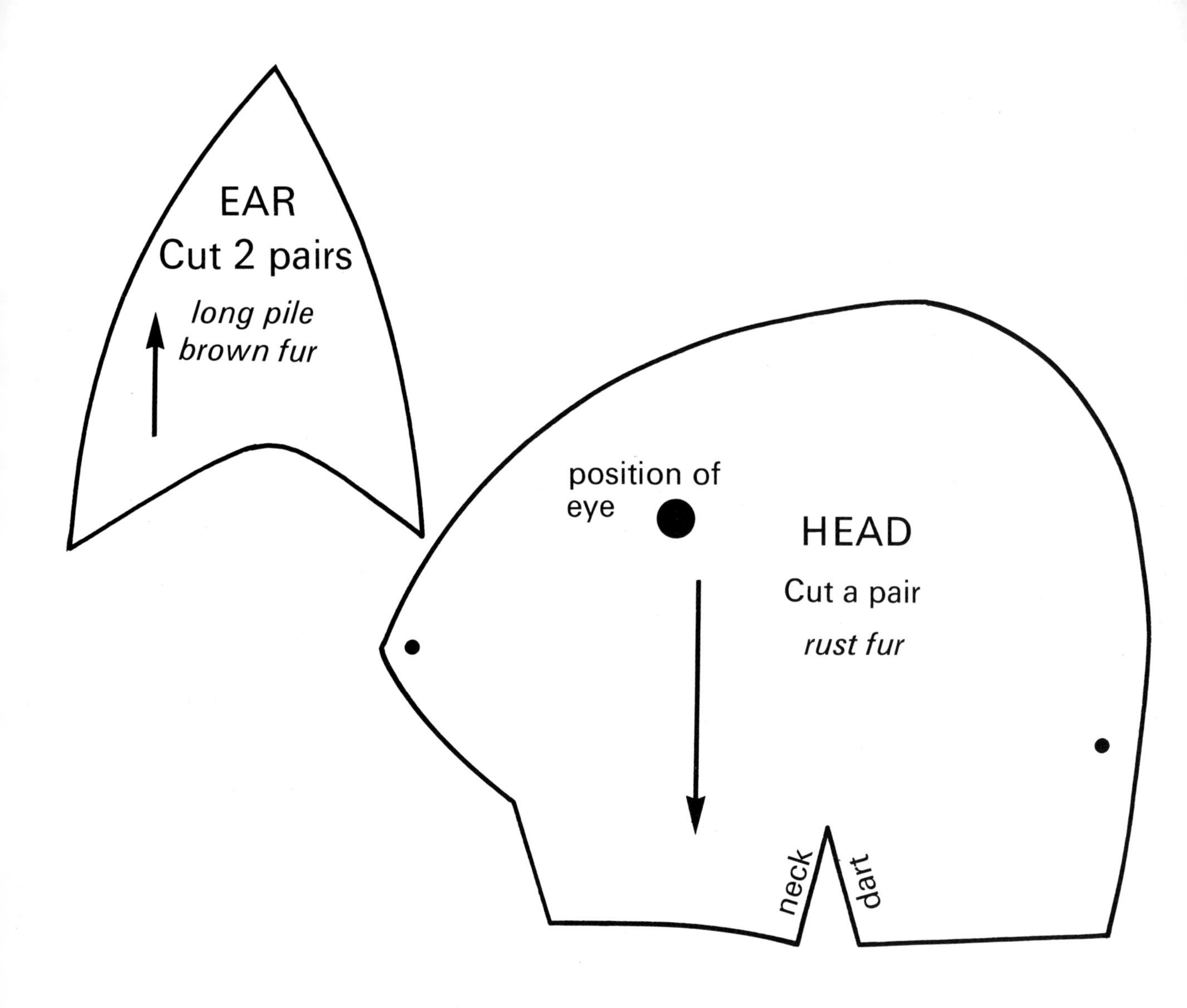

In addition you will need to use the following Little Grey Rabbit pattern pieces

Side Body	cut a pair – *rust fur*
Arm	cut two pairs – *rust fur*
Front Body	cut one – *rust fur*
Base	cut one – *rust fur*
Sole	cut a pair – *beige velour*
Petticoat	cut all pieces from *white cotton*
Dress	cut bodice front and back, sleeves and skirt from *pink cotton*
	cut neck bias after determining the exact length needed

Making the body

1 Squirrel has the same body pattern as Little Grey Rabbit, apart from the bushy tail and a slightly different shaped head and ears. Follow the instructions given for making Little Grey Rabbit through steps 1 to 8. You will find that Squirrel sits comfortably without having to shave any fur away from the base.

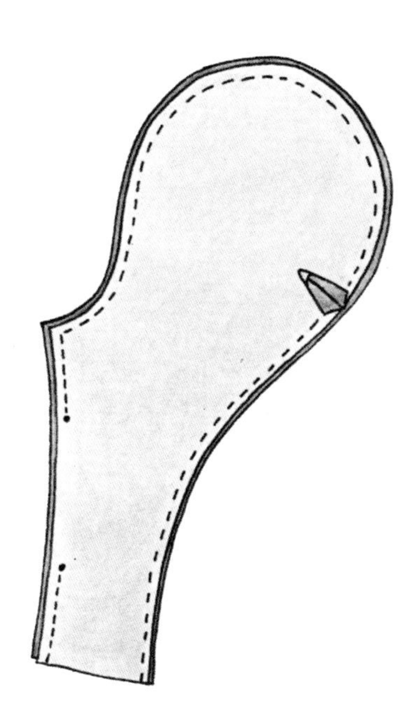

2 Make the small dart in each tail piece first then place them right sides together and sew from the upper match point on the centre back around curve to base. Leave straight edge of base open. Sew lower section of centre back seam from match point down to base.

3 Bring seams at base of tail together centrally, press seam allowance open and sew across to close.

4 Turn tail right side out through opening in centre back seam and lightly stuff the top section only. Hold the stuffing in place by anchoring a thread at X on the back seam and passing the needle through the tail to X on the other side then back again to the start. Pull up tight and fasten off.

5 Position bottom of tail against the base of the body so that it is evenly placed on either side of the centre back seam. Ladder stitch securely in place. When the tail is lifted up, the tail and body centre back seams lie together.

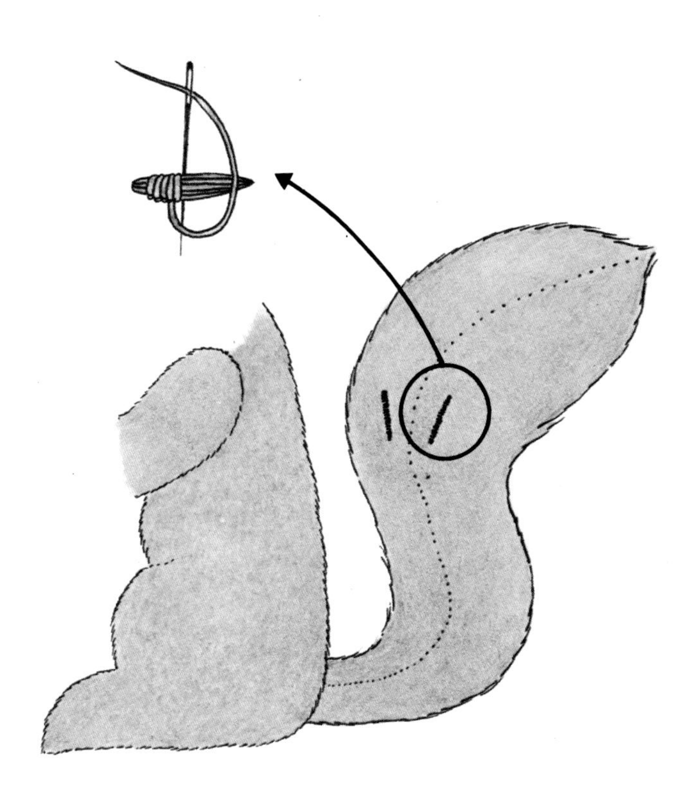

6 Work two buttonhole bars on the tail. The velvet waist ribbon of the dress will thread through these bars and hold the tail up. Each bar is made by working three or four long stitches on the surface at the position marked on the pattern. The stitches are then bound with buttonhole stitch to make a strong, durable loop.

7 Make arms in the same way as described for Little Grey Rabbit (*step 11*) and attach to the body with tape hinges.

8 Make the small dart on the neck edge of both head pieces then finish the head as described for Little Grey Rabbit (*steps 12 – 14*) and ladder stitch to the body.

9 Sew a pair of ear pieces together leaving the bottom edges open. Turn right side out and oversew raw edges together then fold the ear and catch folded edges together (*see diagram*).

Sew the second ear in the same way but fold it on the opposite side to make a pair.

10 Position ears on head and ladder stitch across the back first then across the front so that the ears sit up.

11 Embroider nose and mouth using all six strands of embroidery thread. Again these features are worked in the same way as described for Little Grey Rabbit (*step 16*).

12 Groom the body by brushing and releasing any fur that might be trapped in the seams. In addition, the ears need trimming at the base so that the tips appear more fluffy.

Now make Squirrel's clothes

THE PETTICOAT

Follow the instructions given for Little Grey Rabbit to make up the petticoat.

THE DRESS

1 Squirrel wears a brown, spotted pink cotton dress, a pattern that you will probably have to make for yourself by using a fabric marker pen. Lay the material out flat on a table top with the right side uppermost. Press to remove any creases. Now lay a measure along the lower edge of the fabric and make a foundation row of spots. Each spot in the row should be

38mm ($1\frac{1}{2}$in) apart. Hold the pen vertical for a clean, regular sized spot and allow each completed row-time to dry before marking the next row.

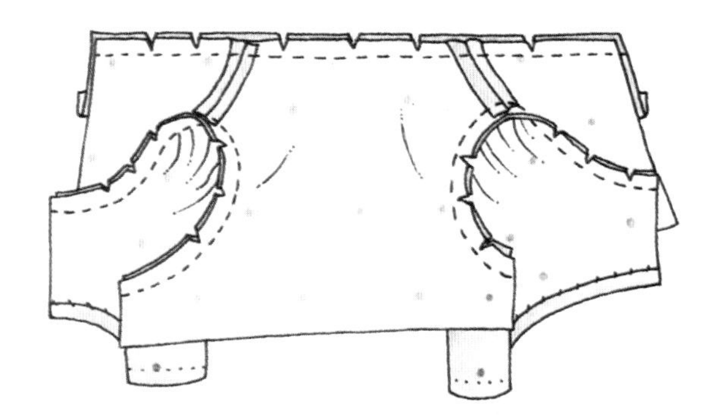

2 Turn the measure at right angles to the foundation row and working from right to left, make vertical rows of spots. The spots in each vertical row should be 5cm (2in) apart.

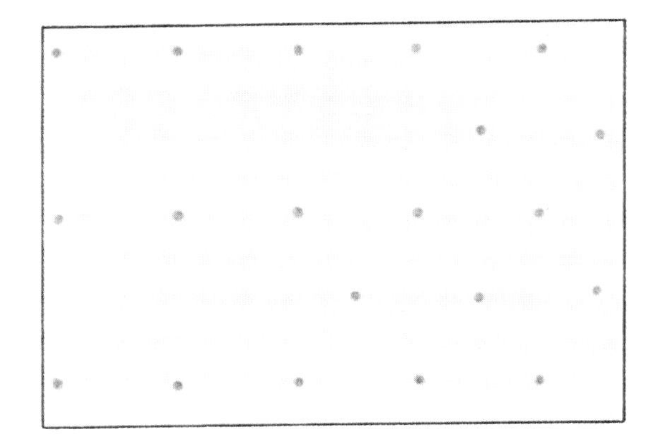

4 Make the dress in the same way as described for Little Grey Rabbit, ignoring instructions for the white cuffs, collar and pin tuck along the lower edge of the skirt. Remember to check that the neck opening fits your toy and make any adjustments at this stage. The size of the neck may mean that you will have to cut a slightly longer neck bias strip.

3 The spot pattern is completed by filling in the inbetween rows which produce the alternating spaced spots. This can be done either by eye or by placing the measure diagonally across the spots already made and spotting the spaces centrally. Make a trial on paper if you want to check the sequence out before marking your fabric. The resulting pattern has horizontal rows 25mm (1in) apart with the spots alternating. Fix the spots by pressing with a hot iron for the length of time recommended by the manufacturers of the fabric.

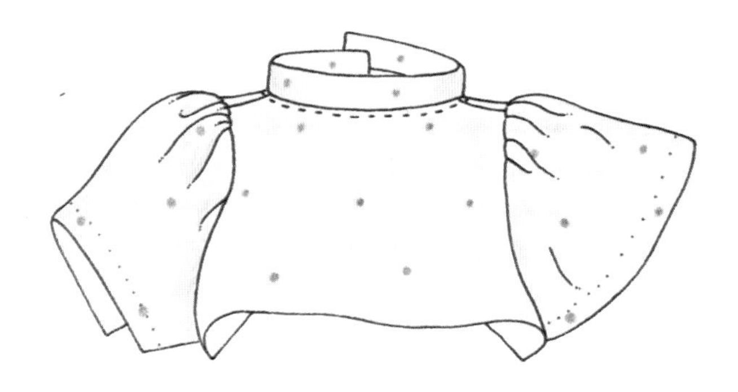

5 Neaten one long edge of neck bias and sew to neck edge of bodice as described for Little Grey Rabbit. Now fold bias down to inside, but leave just enough showing on the right side to make an edging. Hold in place by stitching bodice and bias together close to neck edge.

6 Neaten back edges of dress and fit on Squirrel to determine length before hemming lower edge. Sew press studs at neck and waist to fasten dress at back.

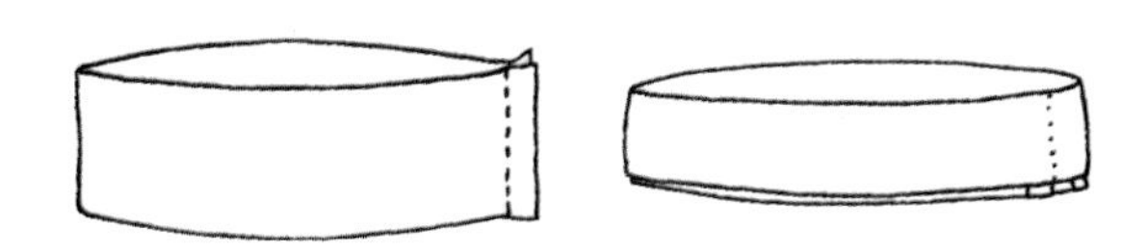

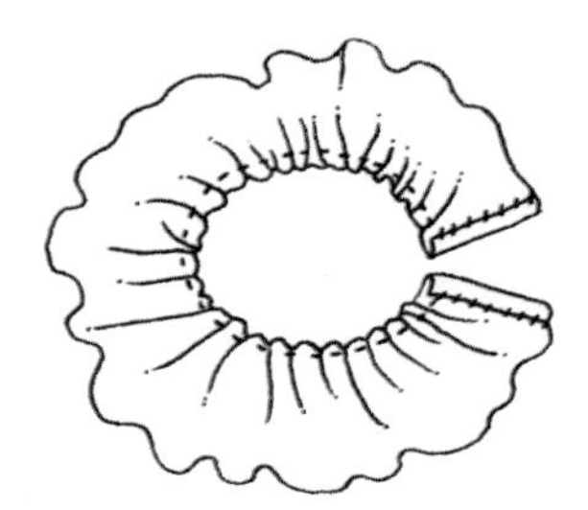

7 Cut the yellow ribbon in half to make the neck frill and the remaining piece in half again to make the two cuff frills. Hem both short ends of the neck ribbon and then gather one long edge to fit neck edge of dress. Hem in place.

8 Sew short ends of a cuff ribbon together then fold ribbon in half with seam to the inside. Gather folded edge and pull up to fit wrist edge of sleeve, hem in place. Make second cuff in the same way.

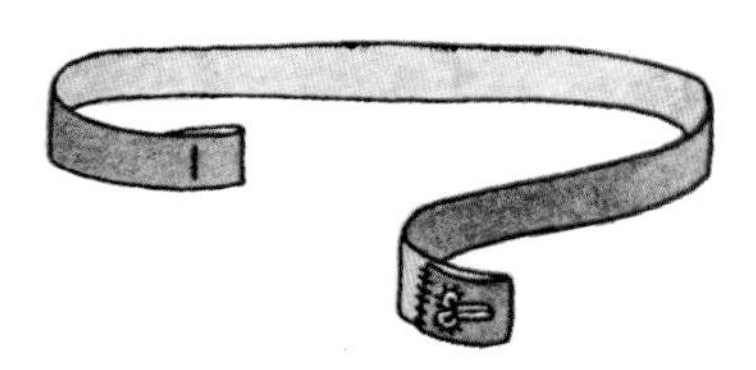

9 Turn under and hem each end of the brown velvet waist ribbon. Sew a hook on one end. Place ribbon around waist so that ends overlap, mark position of overlap and work a small buttonhole bar for the hook. Sew ribbon to dress at side seam so that the hook end fastens on the opposite side under an arm. Finish dressing Squirrel by threading the ribbon through the loops on the tail before fastening.

Old Hedgehog

Materials

For the body – height 25.5cm (10in)

1 Hedgehog fur with a pile depth of 25mm (1in)
30.5cm of 137cm wide fabric ($\frac{1}{3}$yd of 54in) (this is sufficient to make two animals)
2 Dark brown velour for soles and ears
15cm (6in) square
3 Brown tape 22cm (9in) long, 25mm (1in) wide
4 Scrap of shiny black material to make nose

For the clothes

5 Lightweight calico for smock
46cm of 92cm wide fabric ($\frac{1}{2}$yd × 36in)
6 Off-white embroidery thread
7 Red cotton with white spot pattern
30.5cm (12in) square

Also:
150g (6oz) of stuffing
A pair of 14mm brown safety eyes
Nylon thread for whiskers
One hook

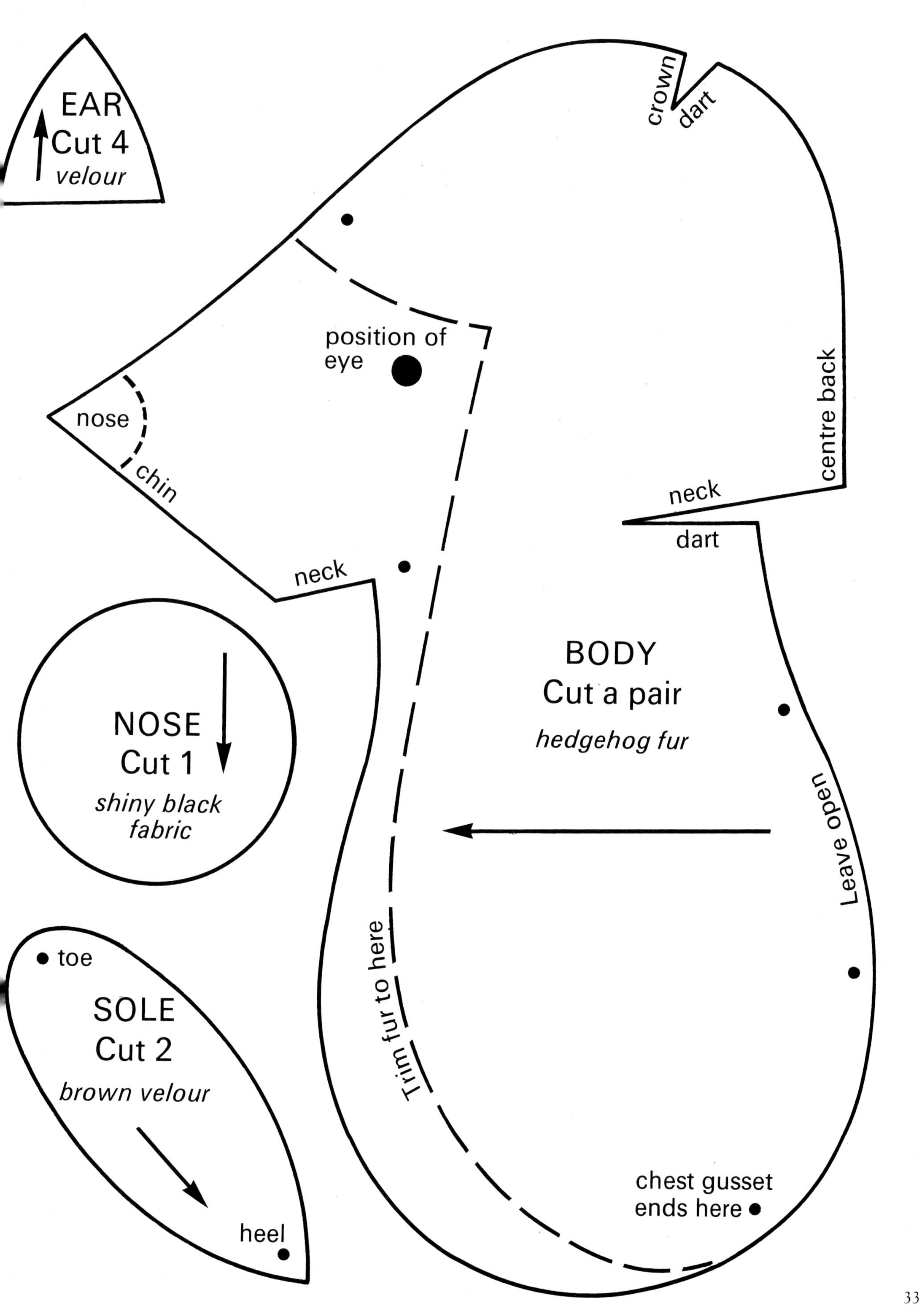
EAR
Cut 4
velour
crown
dart
position of
eye
nose
chin
neck
centre back
neck
dart
BODY
Cut a pair
hedgehog fur
NOSE
Cut 1
shiny black
fabric
Leave open
Trim fur to here
toe
SOLE
Cut 2
brown velour
heel
chest gusset
ends here

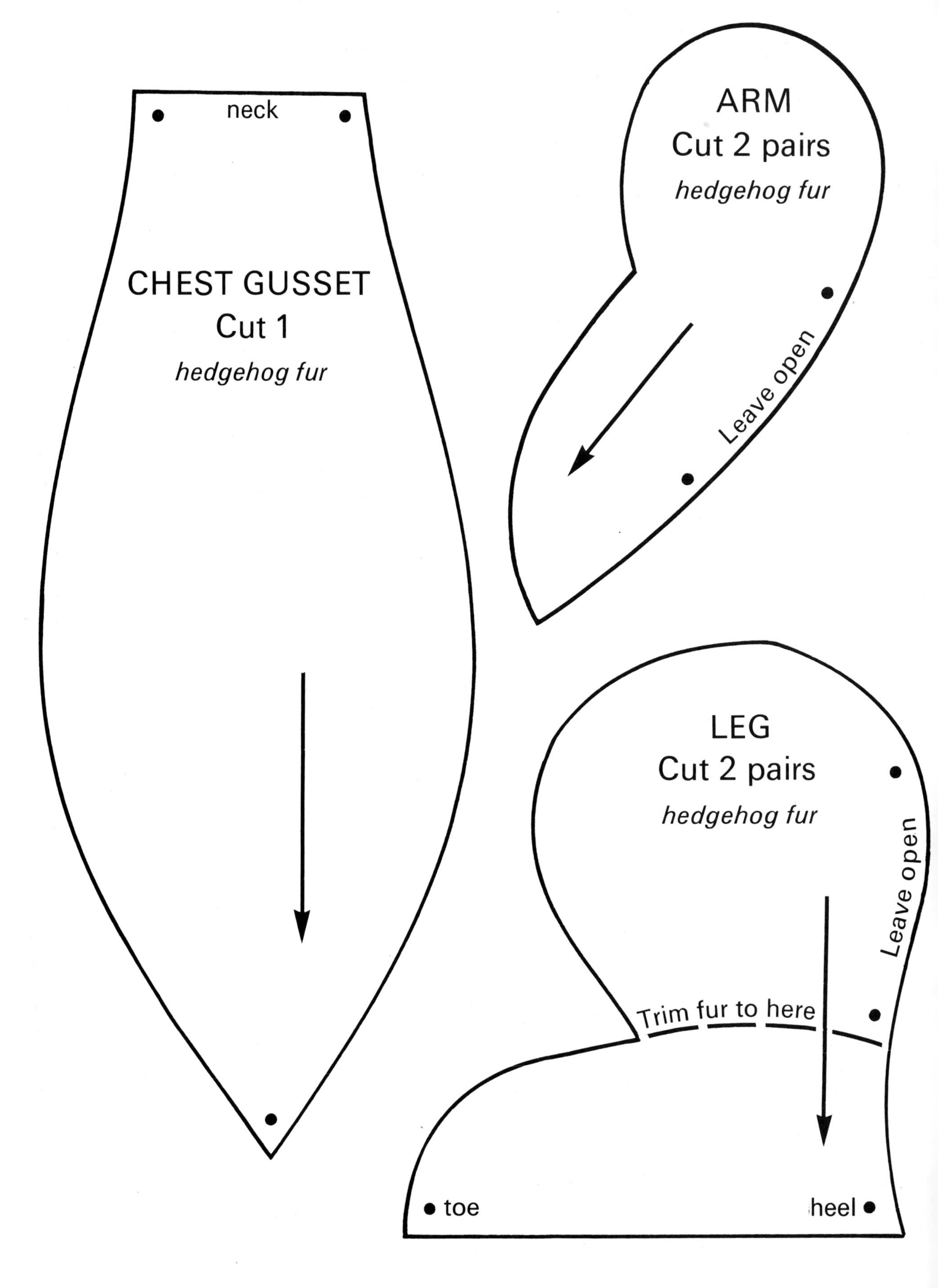
neck
CHEST GUSSET
Cut 1
hedgehog fur
ARM
Cut 2 pairs
hedgehog fur
Leave open
LEG
Cut 2 pairs
hedgehog fur
Leave open
Trim fur to here
toe
heel

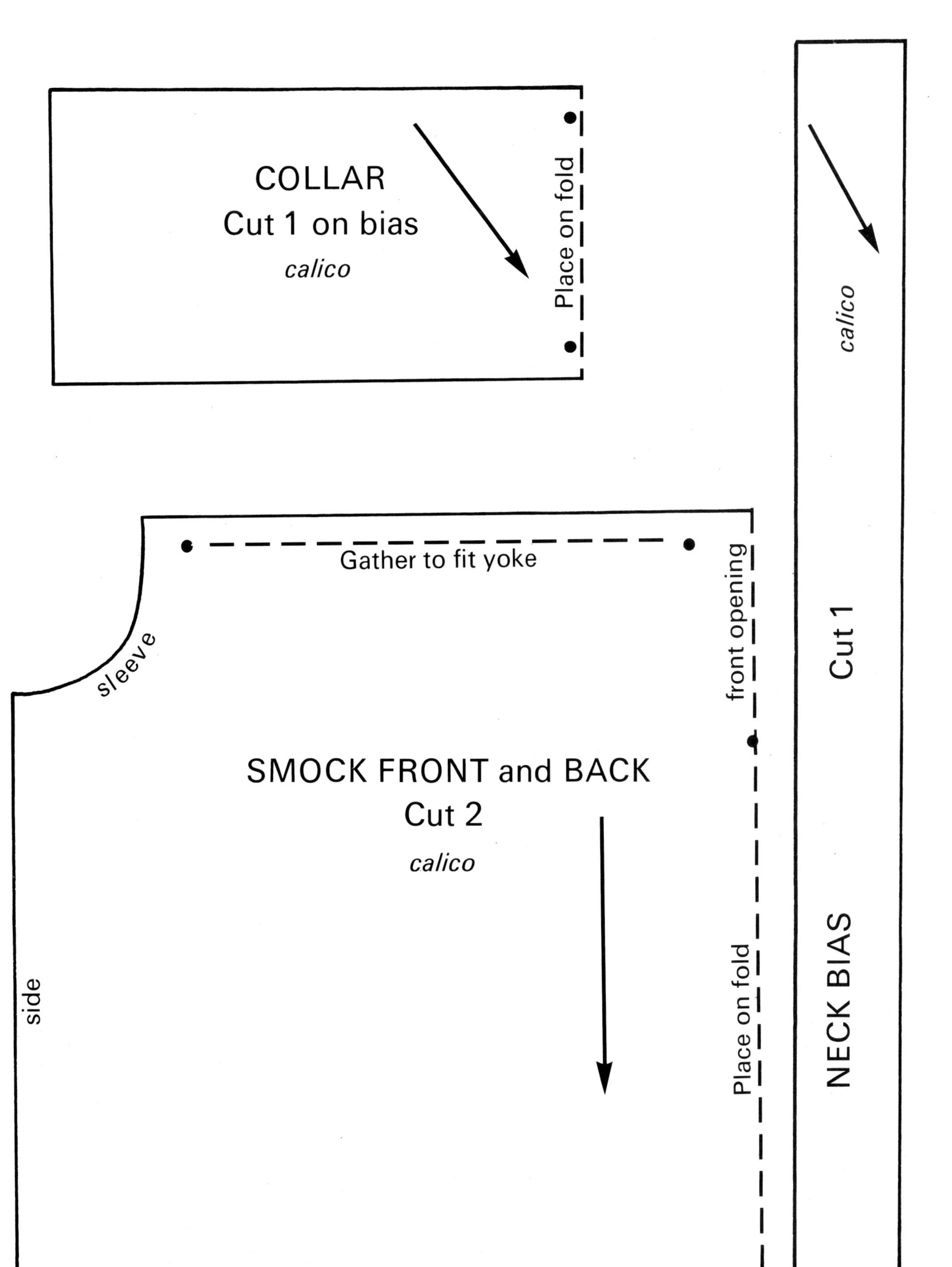
COLLAR
Cut 1 on bias
calico
Place on fold
NECK BIAS
Cut 1
calico
Gather to fit yoke
sleeve
front opening
SMOCK FRONT and BACK
Cut 2
calico
side
Place on fold

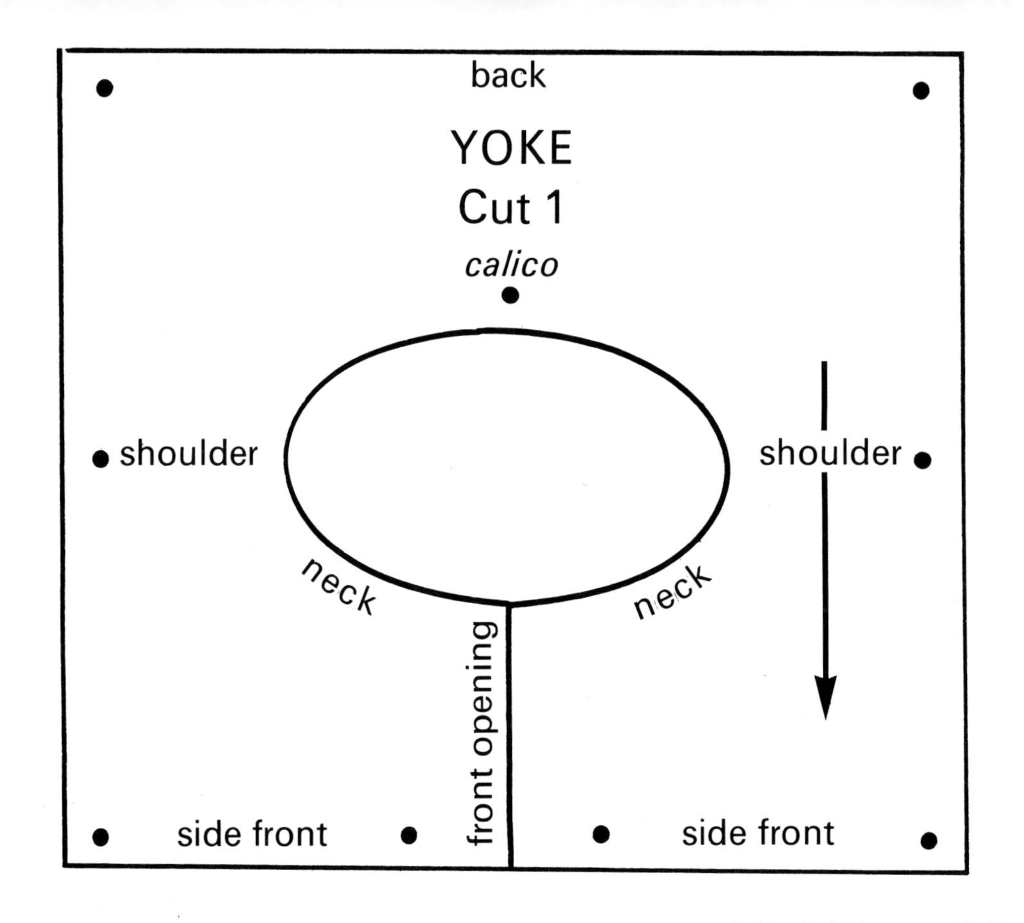

NECKSCARF
Cut a 30.5cm (12in) square of *red cotton* with white spots

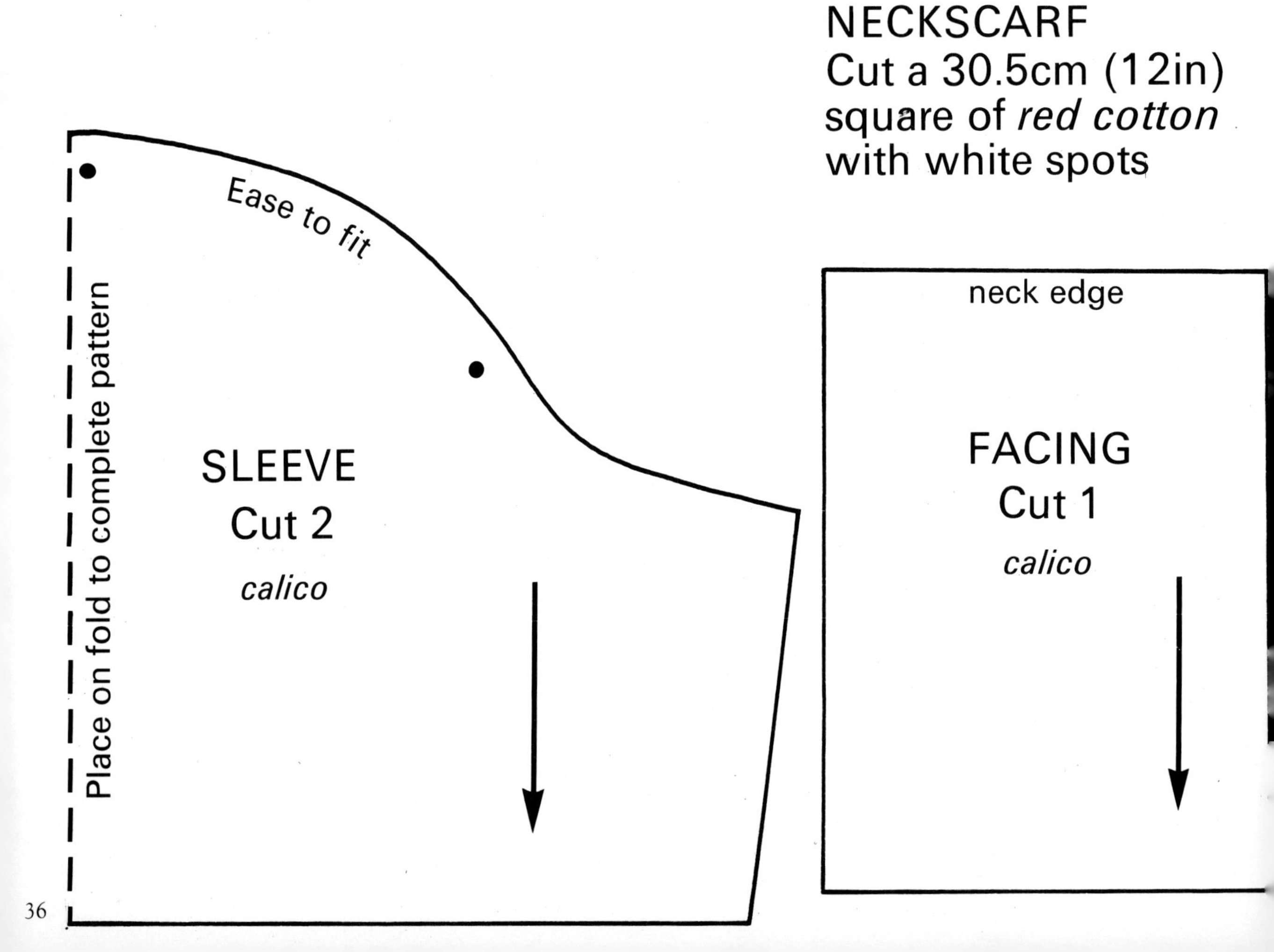

Making the body

1 Prepare all the fur pieces by first trimming the pile away from the seam allowance and then from the entire chest gusset and inside arms so that the fur is short and velvet smooth. Now trim the pile away from the face and front edge of both body pieces up to the line marked on the pattern. The outside arms have the pile trimmed from the paws while the legs should be trimmed so that the pile gradually tapers down to velvet smooth feet (*see picture*).

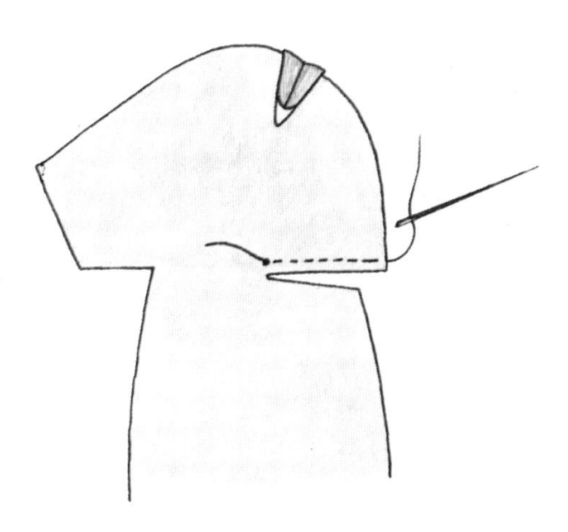

2 Sew the small crown dart on the top of the head, then gather the long edge of the neck dart and pull up to fit the short edge before sewing. Sew the same two darts on the other body piece.

3 Fit the chest gusset between the body pieces and working on one side at a time sew from match points at neck down to lower match point.

4 Sew chin seam from nose to neck edge. Finger press seam open and

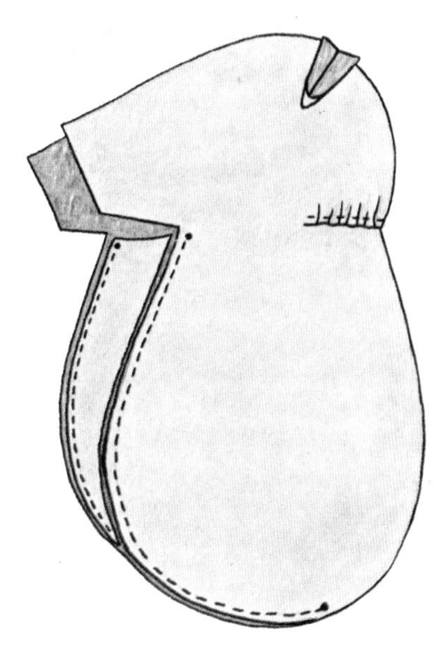

lay neck edge against neck edge of chest gusset and sew. Sew heads together from nose back to match point.

5 Turn skin to right side and finish shaving any long pile from the face to give a pleasing appearance. Fix eyes in place. Turn skin inside out and finish sewing bodies together from head back to opening on centre back and below the opening to the bottom edge of the chest gusset. Turn completed skin right side out, stuff firmly and then close the opening with ladder stitch.

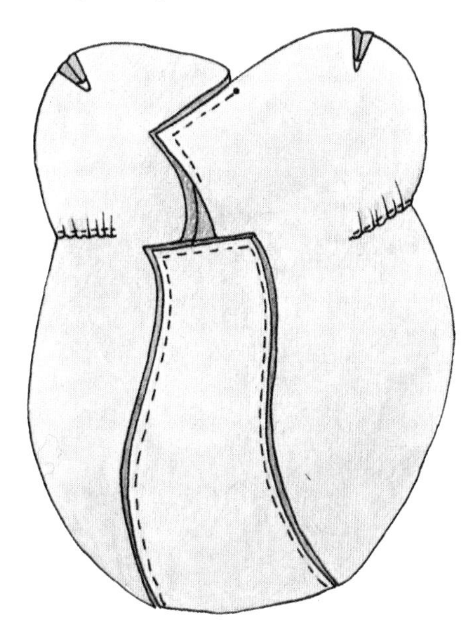

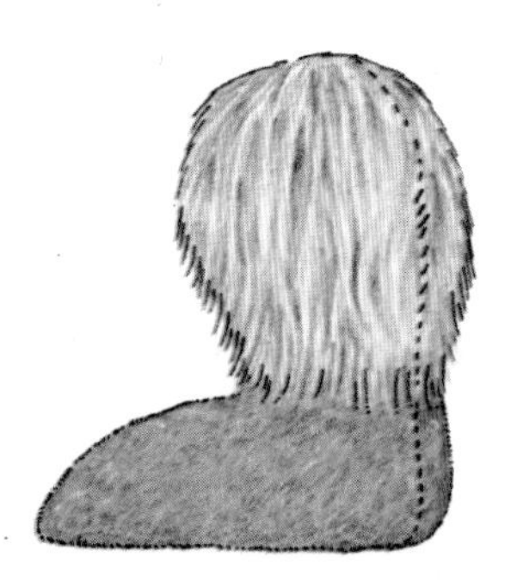

6 Sew legs together in pairs leaving open on the back edge as marked and along the lower straight edge. Insert soles matching toes and heels. Tack in place before sewing. Turn each leg right side out, stuff firmly and close opening.

7 Place legs against body and move around until you are happy with the stance, then ladder stitch in place. Check that feet are level and that Old Hedgehog stands steady.

8 Make arms in the same way as described for Little Grey Rabbit and attach to the body with tape hinges.

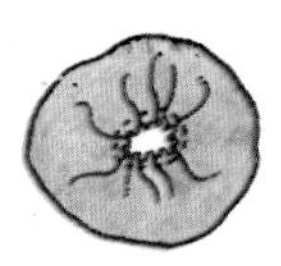

9 Gather edge of nose circle and pull up tight, drawing gathers to centre, which becomes the wrong side. Fold nose in half with right sides together and sew a small dart on each side.

10 Turn nose right side out and pin in position on snout of Hedgehog so that darts appear as nostrils. Hem in place, inserting a little stuffing for shaping as necessary.

11 Sew ears together in pairs with a very narrow seam leaving open at the base. Turn ears right side out, fold raw edges under and sew sides together.

12 Place an ear against the side of the head to find the best position then lay it down flat with the tip facing backwards. Ladder stitch the front side of the ear to the body first which will pull it up and forwards. Then ladder stitch the back side of the ear to the head to pull it back and sink the base down in the pile.

13 Work a few whiskers on each cheek and cut them short, about 25mm (1in) long.

14 Groom Old Hedgehog by brushing the pile backwards and vigorously to raise it up like prickles. Trim any unwanted long pile.

Now make Old Hedgehog's clothes

THE NECKSCARF

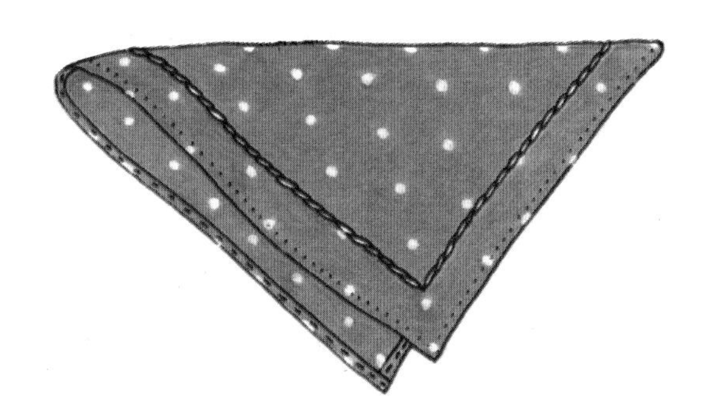

Make a narrow, double hem on all sides of the neckscarf. With white thread, either on the machine or by hand, sew a row of straight stitch 25mm (1in) in from the edge.

THE SMOCK

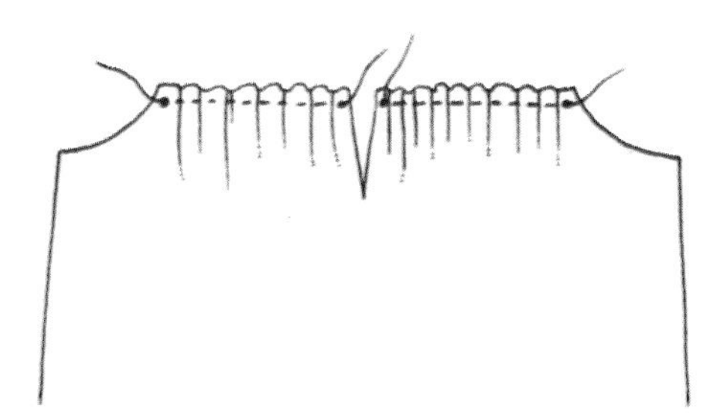

1 Take one of the smock pieces and cut a slit down the centre fold to the match point marked on the fold lines. This piece now becomes the smock front. Gather each top edge either side of the slit and between the match points. Pull up to fit respective side fronts of the yoke.

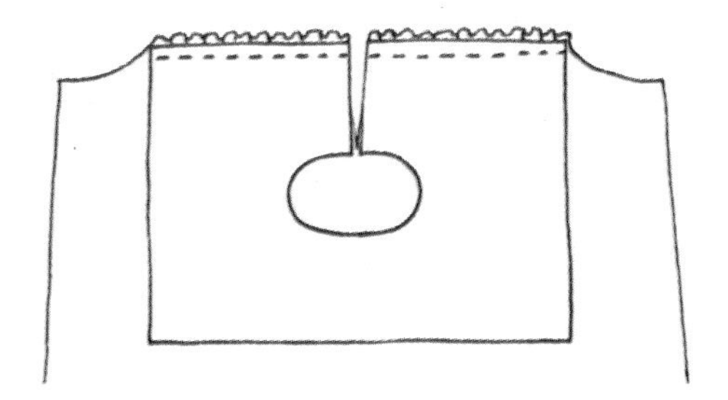

2 With right sides together, sew smock front to yoke on each side. Trim seams and press seam allowance towards the yoke.

3 Neaten facing on both long sides and across bottom edge with a narrow, single hem. Press.

4 Lay right side of facing to front side of smock front having raw edge level with neck edge of yoke. Sew close to the edge down the front opening on each side and across the bottom, squaring off the corners. Slit opening in facing and clip into corners at the bottom.

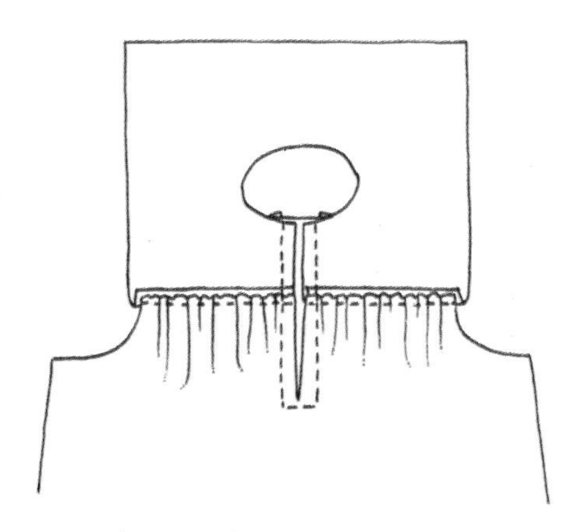

5 Turn facing through slit to wrong side and press. Hold facing down at neck edge by stay stitching all around neck edge.

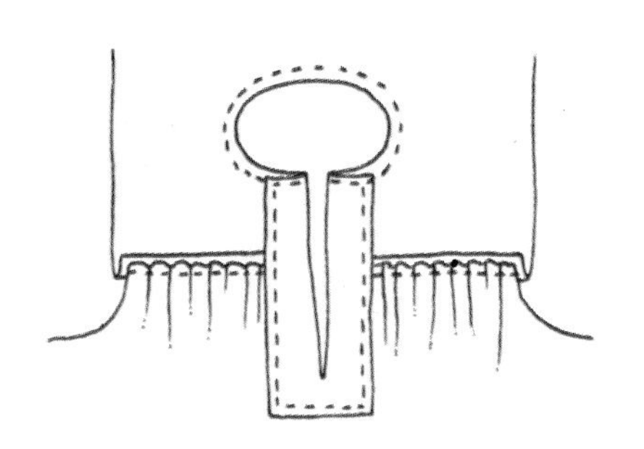

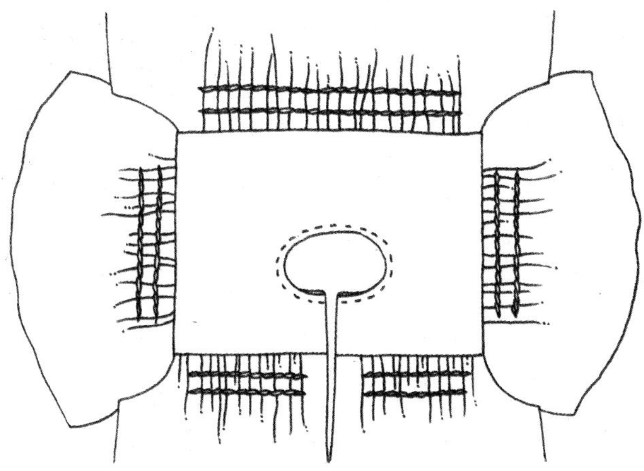

6 Gather width of smock back between match points and pull up to fit yoke. Sew, trim seam allowance then press towards yoke.

7 Gather head of sleeve and pull up to fir smock and yoke opening matching centre of sleeve to shoulder match point. Sew. Trim seam. Make and attach second sleeve to the other side.

8 Imitation smocking is worked by embroidering stem stitch across the gathers of the smock and sleeves. Use three strands of embroidery thread and work 2 rows starting 6mm ($\frac{1}{4}$in) beneath yoke seams on both back and front of smock. The smocking on each sleeve should be a band approximately 25mm (1in) wide and again, 2 rows deep.

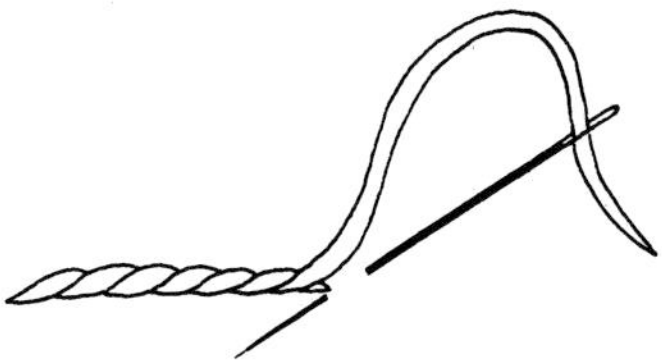

9 Fold collar in half bringing match points together and sew each short end. Trim seams and clip corners. Turn collar right side out and press.

10 Position collar on neck edge of yoke matching centres at the back and having all raw edges level. Sew, trim seam and clip neck edge as shown.

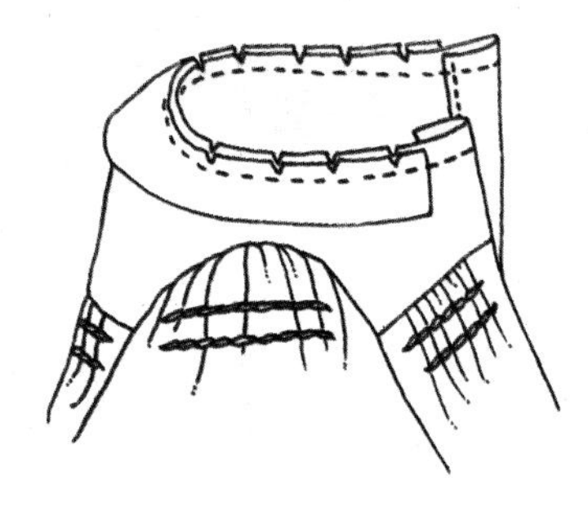

11 Neaten one long edge of neck bias then lay raw edge against neck edge, sew and finish in the same way as described for Little Grey Rabbit's dress (*steps 7 and* 8).

12 Make a narrow double hem at the wrist edge of both sleeves. Sew underarm and side seam of smock on each side

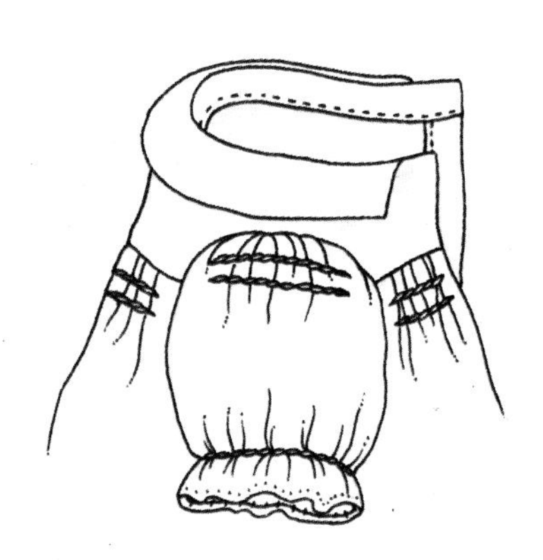

13 Gather lower edge of sleeve just behind the wrist edge and pull up so that it just fits the arm comfortably. Using three strands of embroidery thread, work a single row of stem stitch over the gathering to hold it secure. Finish other sleeve in the same way.

14 Fit smock on Old Hedgehog to determine length before hemming lower edge. Finish smock by sewing a hook on the front opening at the lower edge of the yoke. Work a buttonhole bar on the opposite side of the opening. Finally, fold neckscarf diagonally and tie around the neck.

Weasel

Materials

For the body – height 27cm (10½in)

1 Rust coloured fur with a pile depth of 25mm (1in)
30.5cm of 137cm wide fabric (⅓yd × 54in)
2 Scrap of short pile, dark brown or black polished fur for tail tip
3 Beige velour or velvet for soles
15cm (6in) square
4 Brown tape 22cm (9in) long, 25mm (1in) wide
5 Black embroidery thread for nose

For the clothes

6 Yellow cotton for waistcoat
15cm of 92cm wide fabric (6in × 36in)
7 2 small white buttons
8 Black cotton for coat
46cm of 92cm wide fabric (½yd × 36in)
9 2 small black buttons

Also:
226g (8oz) stuffing
A pair of 16mm brown safety eyes
Nylon thread for whiskers
2 × 7mm press studs
2 × 7mm black press studs

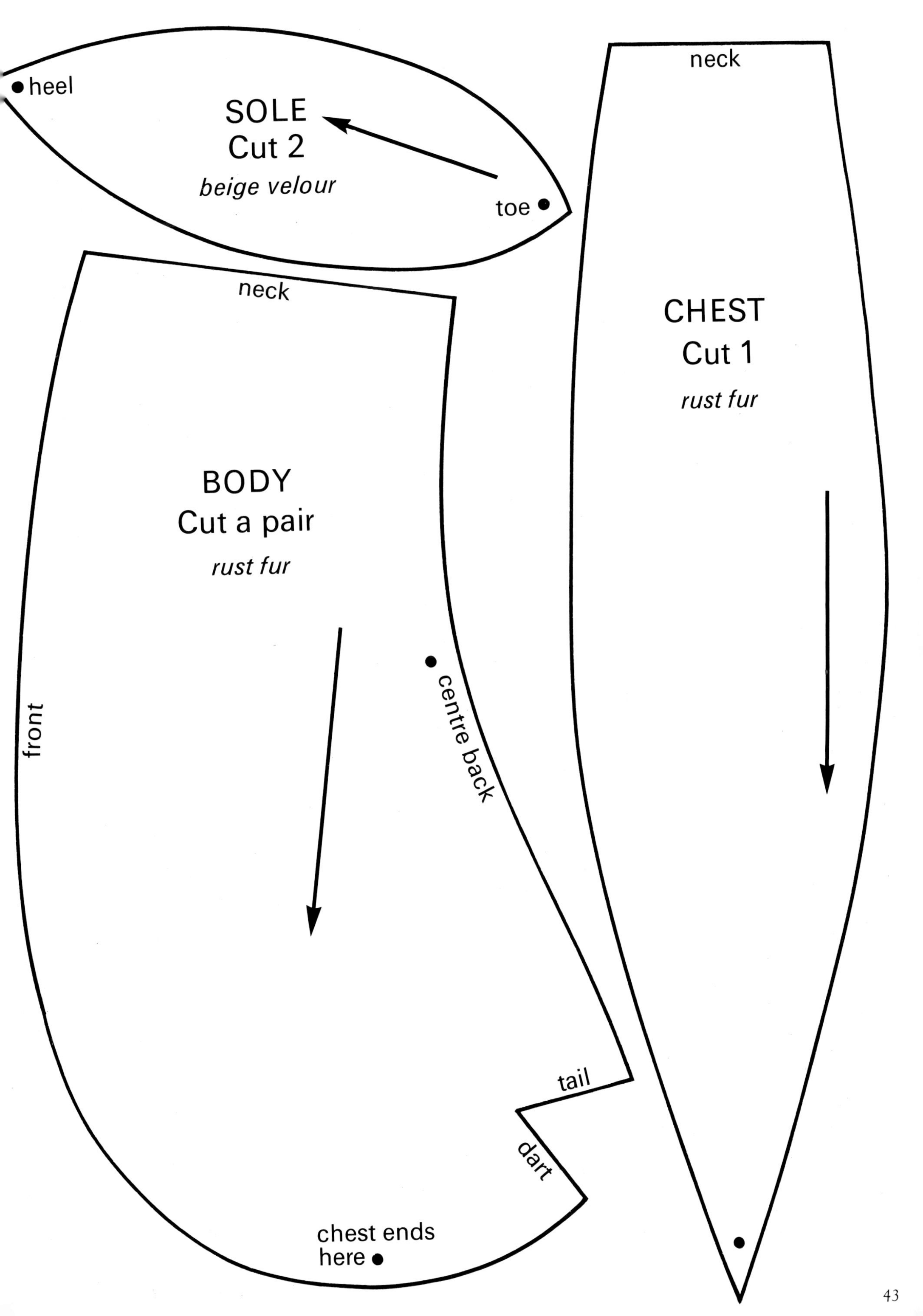
heel
SOLE
Cut 2
beige velour
toe
neck
CHEST
Cut 1
rust fur
neck
BODY
Cut a pair
rust fur
front
centre back
tail
dart
chest ends
here

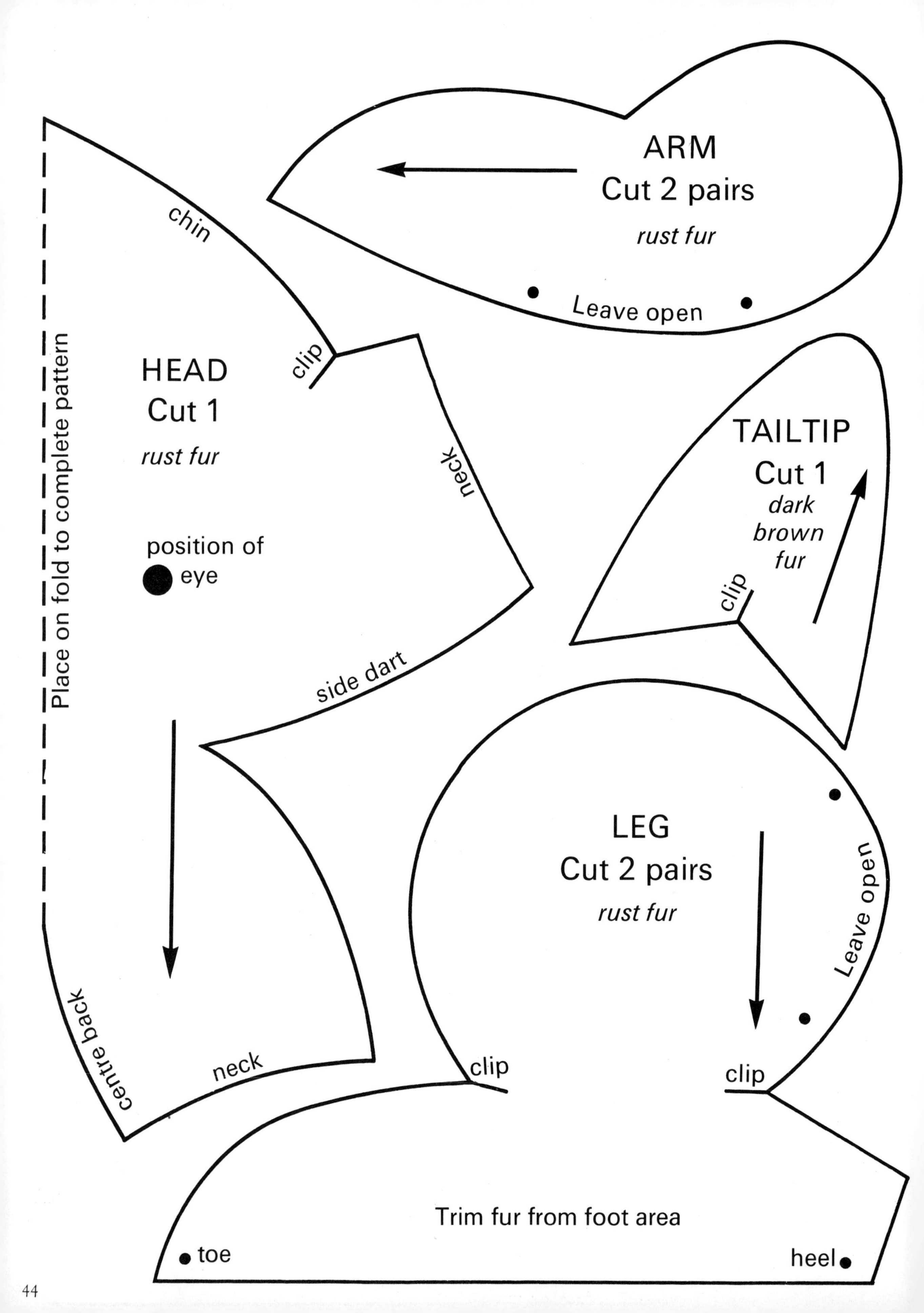
ARM
Cut 2 pairs
rust fur
Leave open
chin
clip
HEAD
Cut 1
rust fur
neck
Place on fold to complete pattern
position of
eye
side dart
TAILTIP
Cut 1
dark
brown
fur
clip
LEG
Cut 2 pairs
rust fur
Leave open
centre back
neck
clip
clip
Trim fur from foot area
toe
heel

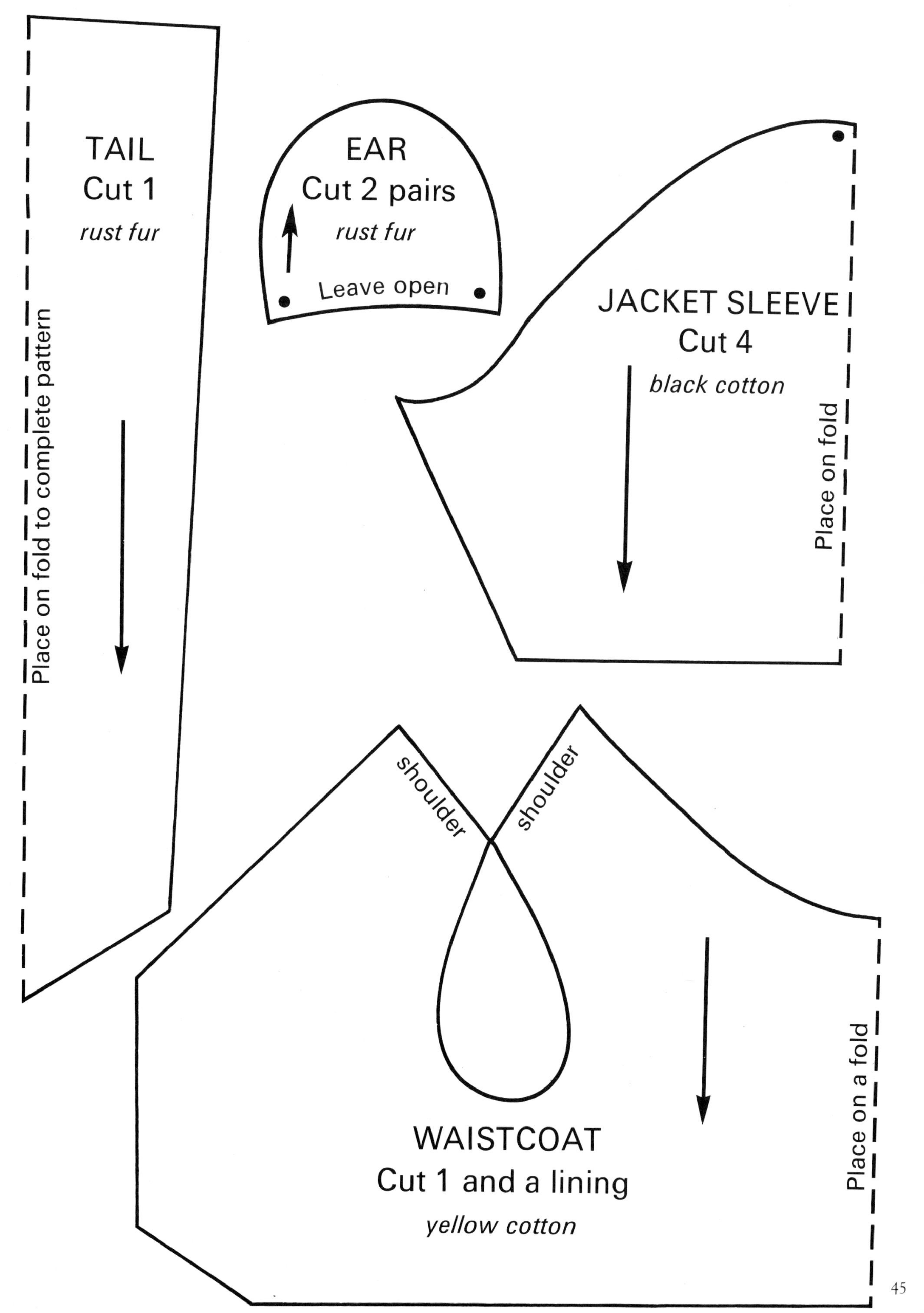
TAIL
Cut 1
rust fur
Place on fold to complete pattern
EAR
Cut 2 pairs
rust fur
Leave open
JACKET SLEEVE
Cut 4
black cotton
Place on fold
shoulder
shoulder
WAISTCOAT
Cut 1 and a lining
yellow cotton
Place on a fold

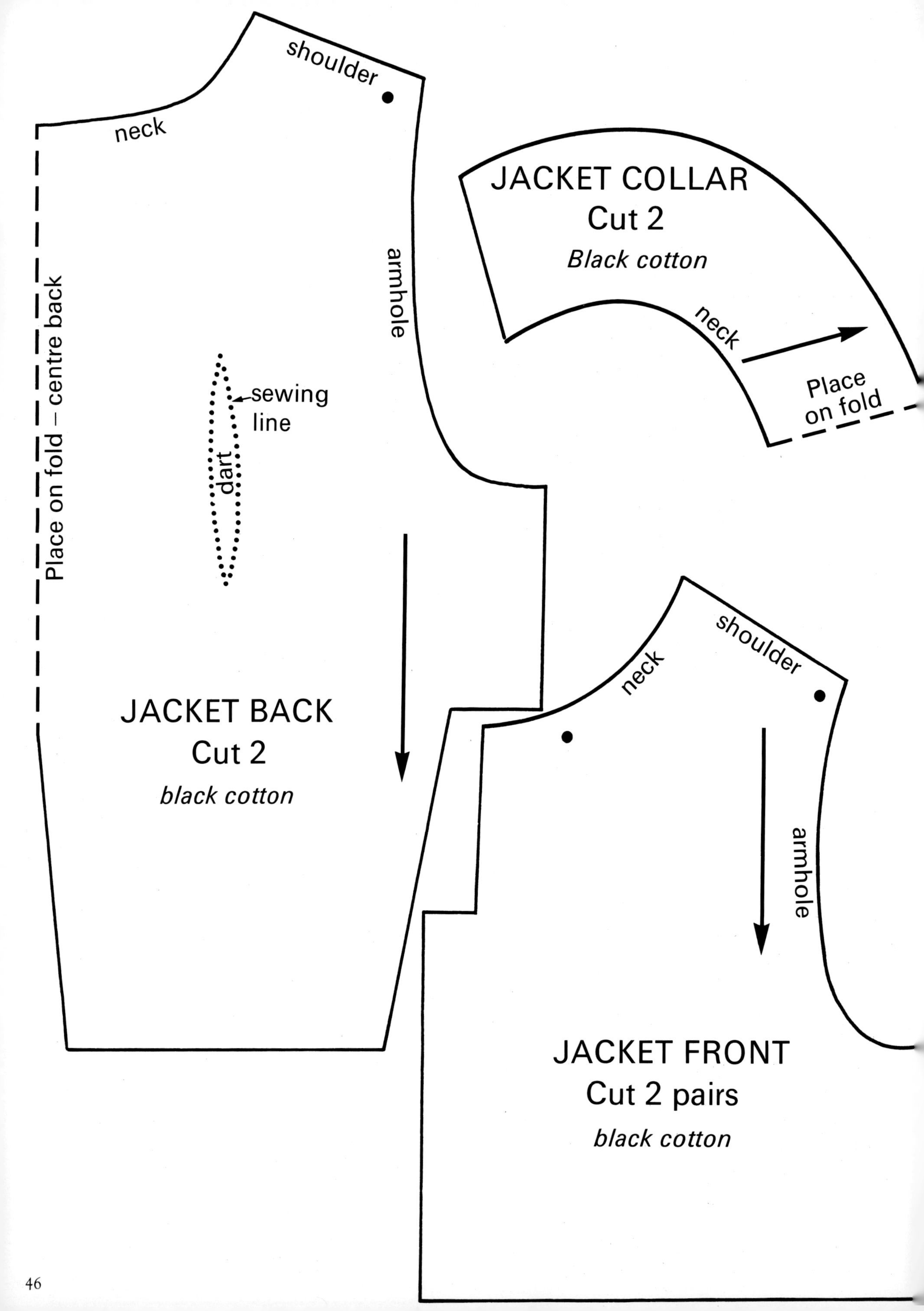
shoulder
neck
armhole
Place on fold – centre back
sewing line
dart
JACKET BACK
Cut 2
black cotton
JACKET COLLAR
Cut 2
Black cotton
neck
Place on fold
shoulder
neck
armhole
JACKET FRONT
Cut 2 pairs
black cotton

Making the body

1 Sew chest to front edge of each side body in turn working from neck edge down to the match point.

2 Sew side bodies together on centre back between the match points on either side of the tail dart.

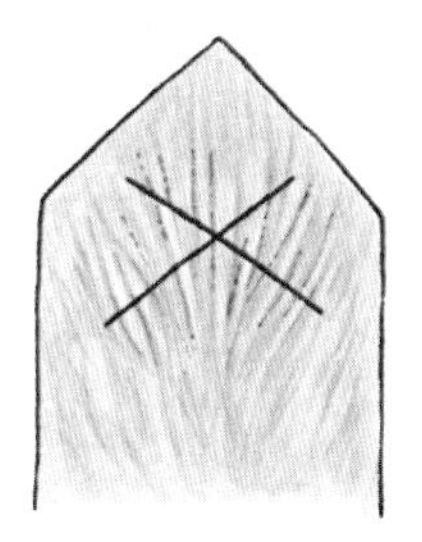

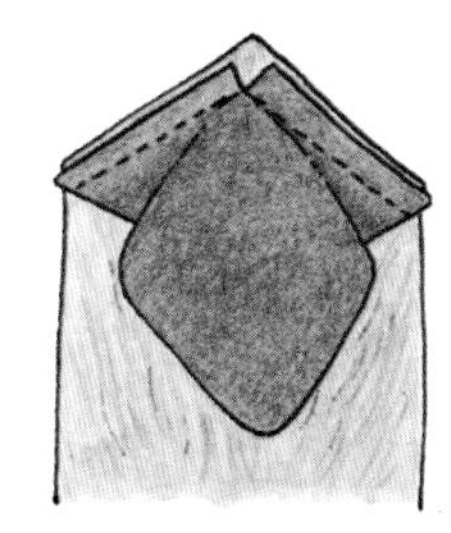

3 Fold fur back from the tip of the rust tail piece and hold down with a large, temporary cross stitch. Place dark brown tail tip over end of rust tail section and with raw edges level, sew across. Cut the cross stitch to release the pile.

4 Fold tail in half lengthways with right sides together and sew from the tip backwards for approximately 5cm (2in). Turn tail right side out and finish closing sides together by hand, using ladder stitch. Brush and groom tail at this stage. Trim some of the fullness of pile away to make a tapered tail. There is no need to stuff the tail.

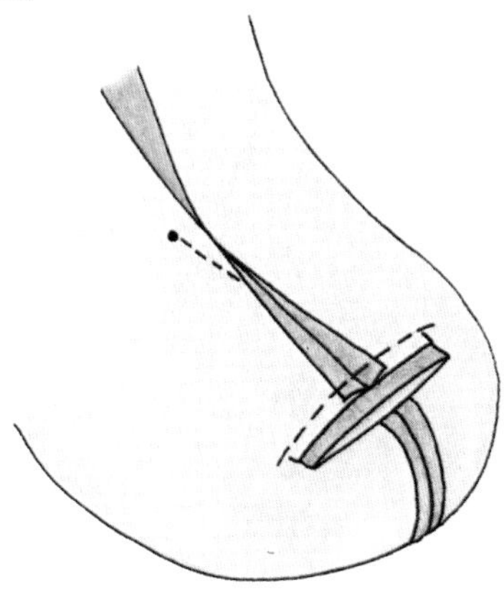

5 Insert tail into body through the tail dart with the tail seam on the underside. When all raw edges are level, sew across several times to secure. Finish sewing centre back seam up to neck edge.

6 Turn body right side out and stuff firmly through the neck opening. Gather neck edge and pull up before fastening off.

7 Make legs in the same way as described for Old Hedgehog (*step 7*) and ladder stitch in place against the side of the body.

8 Make arms as described for Little Grey Rabbit (*step 11*) and sew to the body with tape hinges.

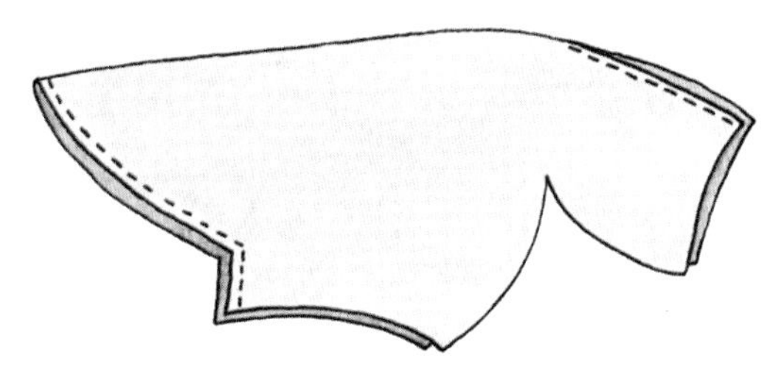

9 Fold head in half to sew the chin seam from nose to neck and the dart on the centre back of the head.

10 Press seam open at nose and sew across 12mm ($\frac{1}{2}$in) back from the tip. Trim point.

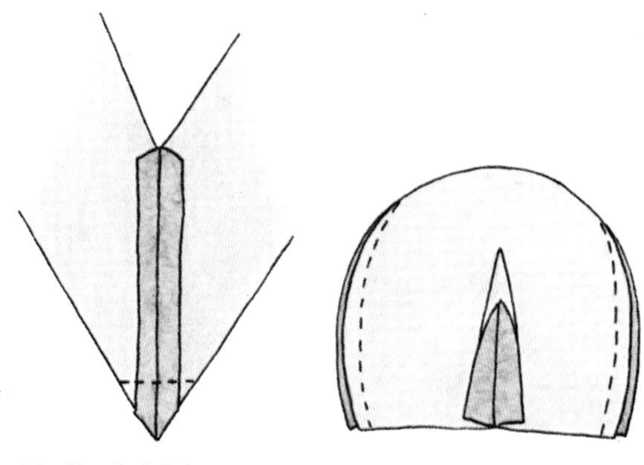

11 Refold head and sew front and back sections together on each side in turn.

12 Turn completed head right side out and insert safety eyes. Stuff head firmly then gather up neck edge at back only, to draw in the fullness. Ladder stitch head to body. Trim pile from around nose and the eyes so that they can be seen.

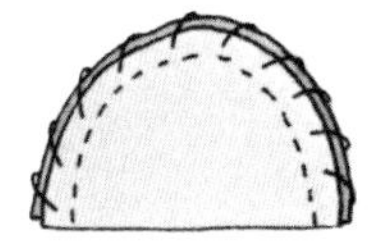

13 Trim the pile from the front ears so that they are velvet smooth. Sew each front ear to a back ear piece after first oversewing the edges together, taking care to tuck the long pile in. Turn ears right side out and oversew bottom edges together pulling up on stitches to narrow the base.

14 Place ears on head and move around to find a pleasing position. Ladder stitch across front side first then across the back which will pull the ears backwards and close in against the head. Trim as necessary.

15 Work a block of satin stitches for the nose and finish with several long whiskers on each cheek.

Now make Weasel's clothes

THE WAISTCOAT

1 Spread both waistcoat pieces out flat with right sides together. Sew all round edge leaving an opening at the centre back waist edge.

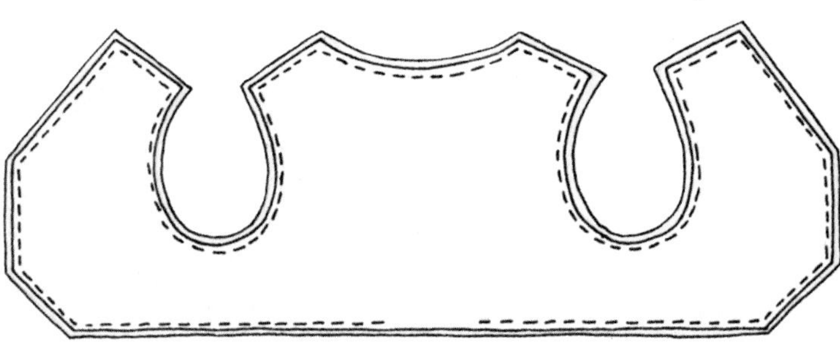

2 Trim all seams, clip corners and curves. Turn waistcoat right side out, press then close opening with a small slip stitch. Fit on Weasel and either butt or overlap shoulders and hem to hold. Sew the two white buttons on the front edge of the waistcoat and instead of working buttonholes sew a press stud under each button.

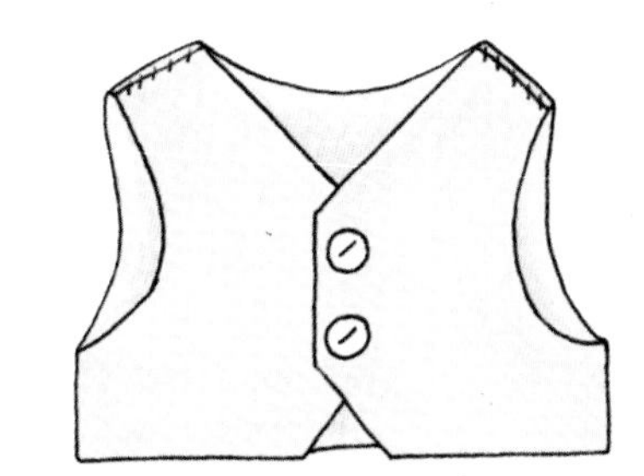

THE JACKET

1 Make the two darts in the jacket back, then sew fronts to back on the shoulders.

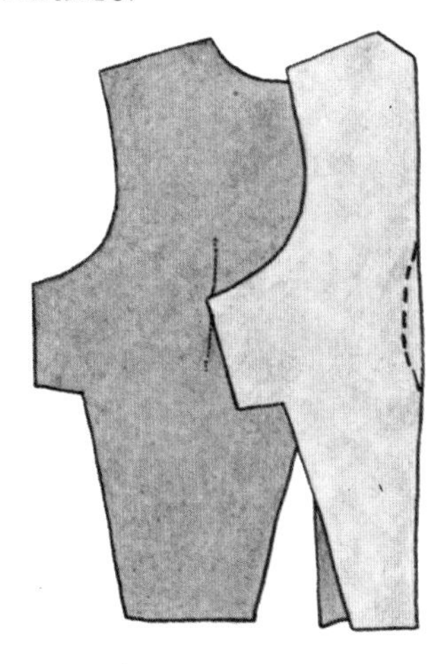

2 Ease head of first sleeve as you sew it to the armhole edge. Trim seam allowance. Fit second sleeve in the same way. Now sew underarm and side seam of jacket on each side in turn.

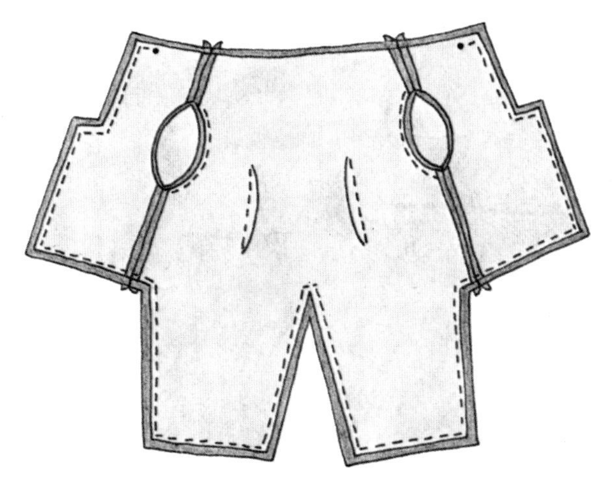

3 Use the second set of front and back jacket pieces and sleeves to make a lining. Prepare in exactly the same way. With right sides together, carefully fit jacket and lining together, matching up seams. Sew together from front neck edge at match point down front and across bottom of tails then up the front on the other side to finish at the neck edge match point. Trim all seams, clip corners off, turn right side out and press.

4 Fit jacket on Weasel to determine sleeve length. Turn raw edges of sleeves under and hem together. This is neater if the outside sleeve is slightly longer than the sleeve lining so that the hemming is back from the edge.

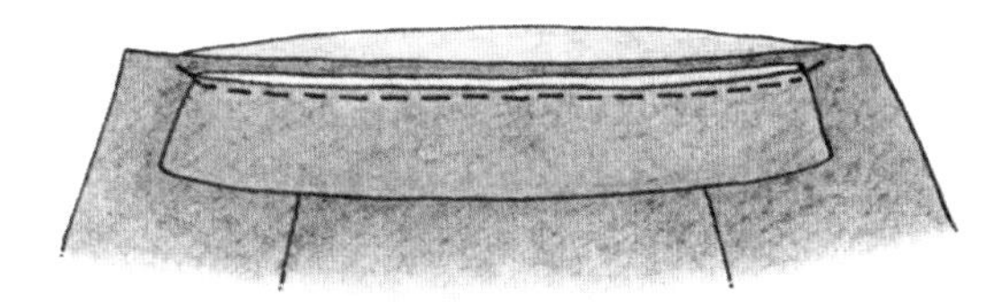

5 Sew collars together leaving neck edge open. Trim seam allowance, turn right side out and press. Sew collar to neck edge of lining, keeping jacket tucked out of the way.

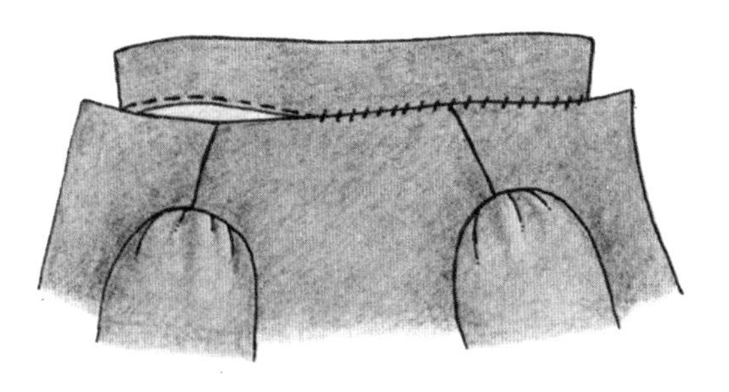

6 Trim neck edge of collar and lining and turn seam allowance to the inside of the jacket. Fold under neck seam allowance of jacket and hem to collar stitching line. This row of stitching will be hidden by the collar as it is rolled over.

7 Sew the black press studs to the front opening of the jacket and then cover them by sewing a black button on top of each press stud.

Materials

For the body – height 46cm (18in)

1 Beige beaver quality fur with a pile depth of 12/13mm ($\frac{1}{2}$in)
46cm of 137cm wide fabric ($\frac{1}{2}$yd × 54in)
2 Brown velour or velveteen for soles
15cm (6in) square
3 Short pile white fur for ear linings
23cm (9in) square
4 White fur for tail with a pile depth of 25mm (1in)
15cm (6in) square
5 Beige tape 22cm (9in) long, 25mm (1in) wide
6 Brown embroidery thread for nose
7 Scrap of brown felt for eye backings

For the clothes

8 White cotton for shirt
30.5cm of 115cm wide fabric ($\frac{1}{3}$yd × 45in)
9 White cotton twill for waistcoat
30.5cm of 92cm wide fabric ($\frac{1}{3}$yd × 36in)
10 Blue wool for coat
40cm of 150cm wide fabric (15in × 60in)
11 Blue cotton for pocket and cuff linings
23cm (9in) square
12 4 white buttons for the waistcoat
13 3 blue buttons for the coat
14 Red herringbone tape 25mm (1in) wide, 54cm (21in) long
15 Gold cord for chain 1m (1yd)
Also:
340g (12oz) stuffing Nylon thread for whiskers
3 × 7mm press studs A small hook
A pair of 16mm brown safety eyes

Hare

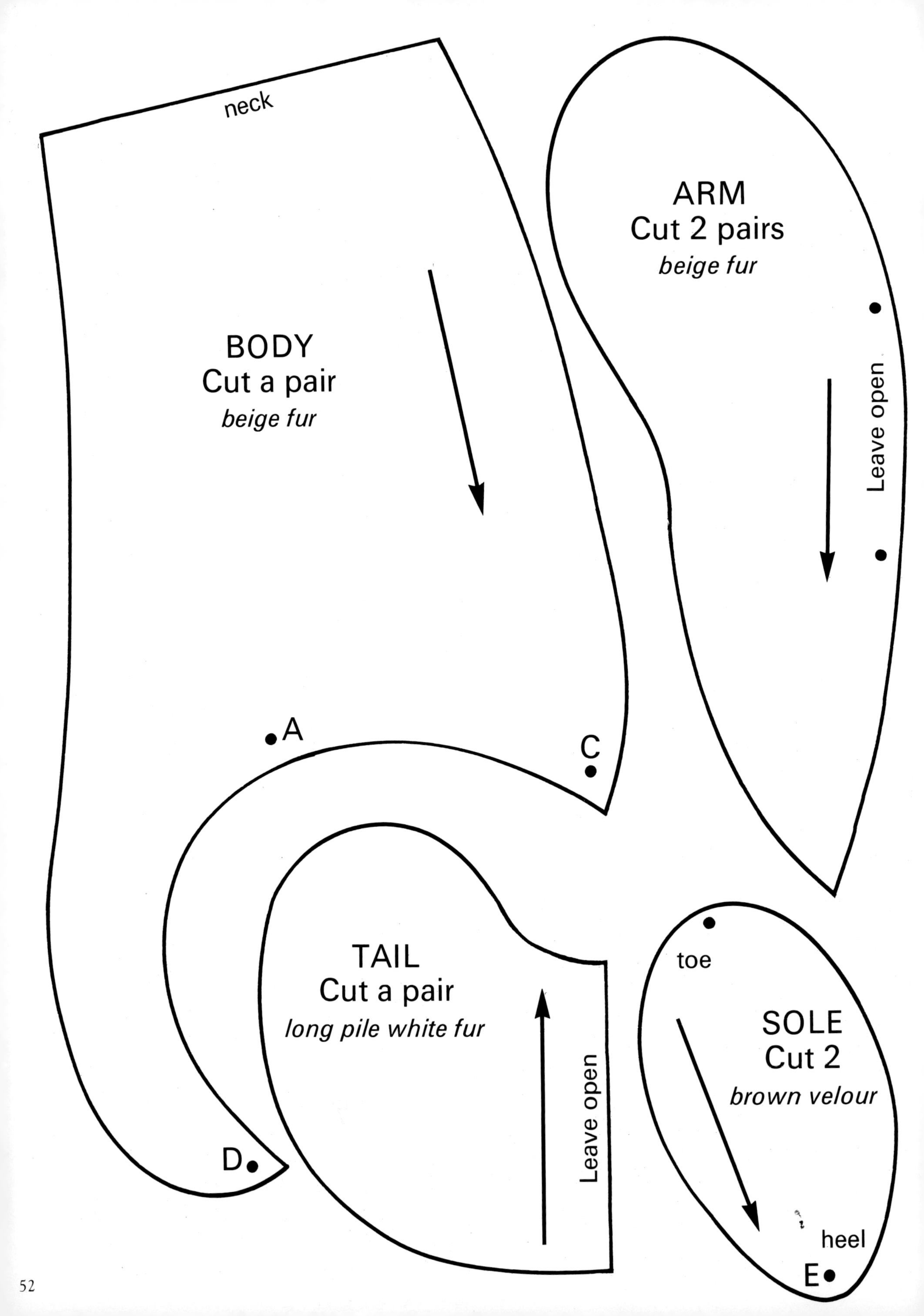
neck
BODY
Cut a pair
beige fur
A
C
D
ARM
Cut 2 pairs
beige fur
Leave open
TAIL
Cut a pair
long pile white fur
Leave open
toe
SOLE
Cut 2
brown velour
heel
E

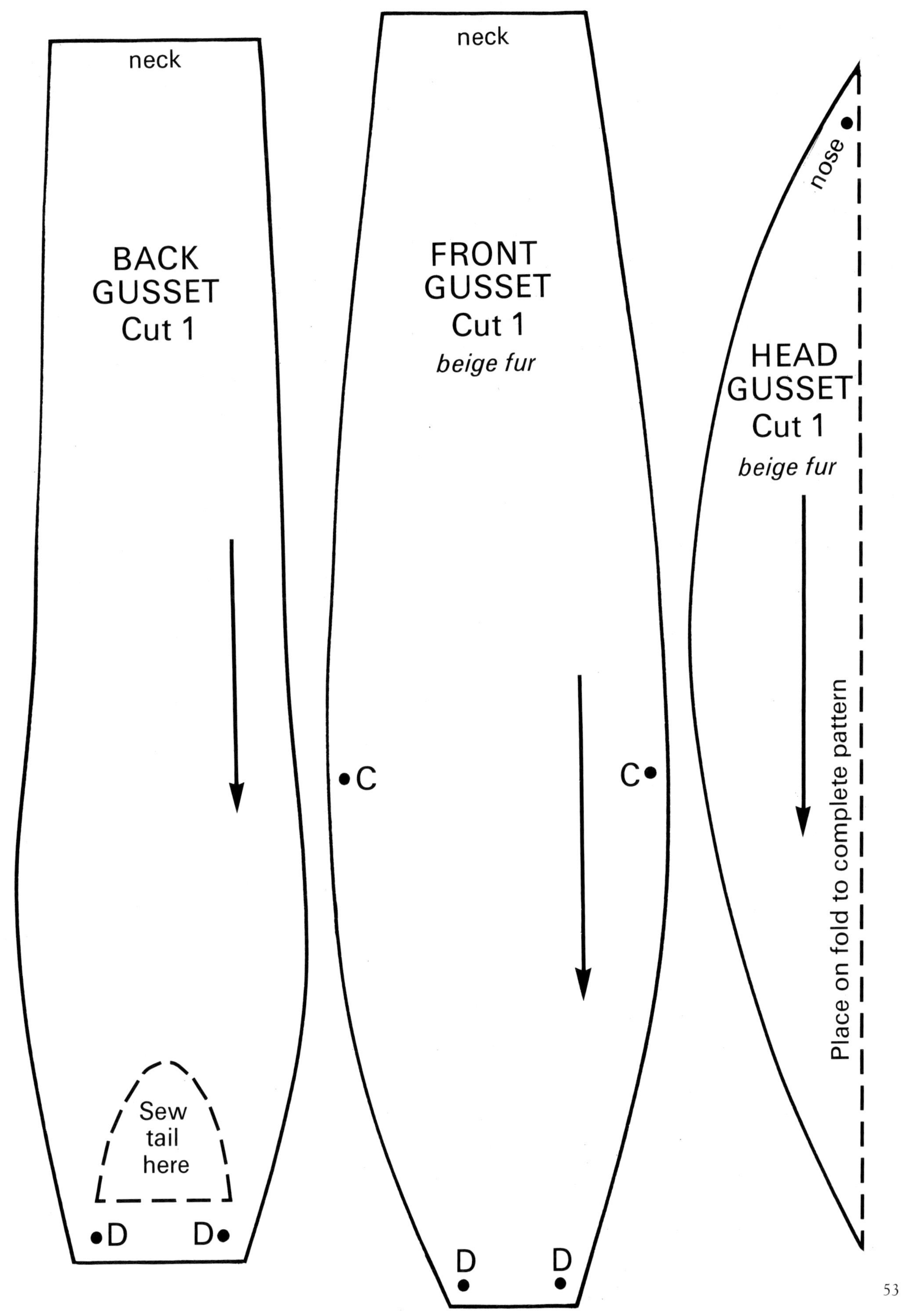
neck
BACK
GUSSET
Cut 1
Sew
tail
here
D
D
neck
FRONT
GUSSET
Cut 1
beige fur
C
C
D
D
nose
HEAD
GUSSET
Cut 1
beige fur
Place on fold to complete pattern

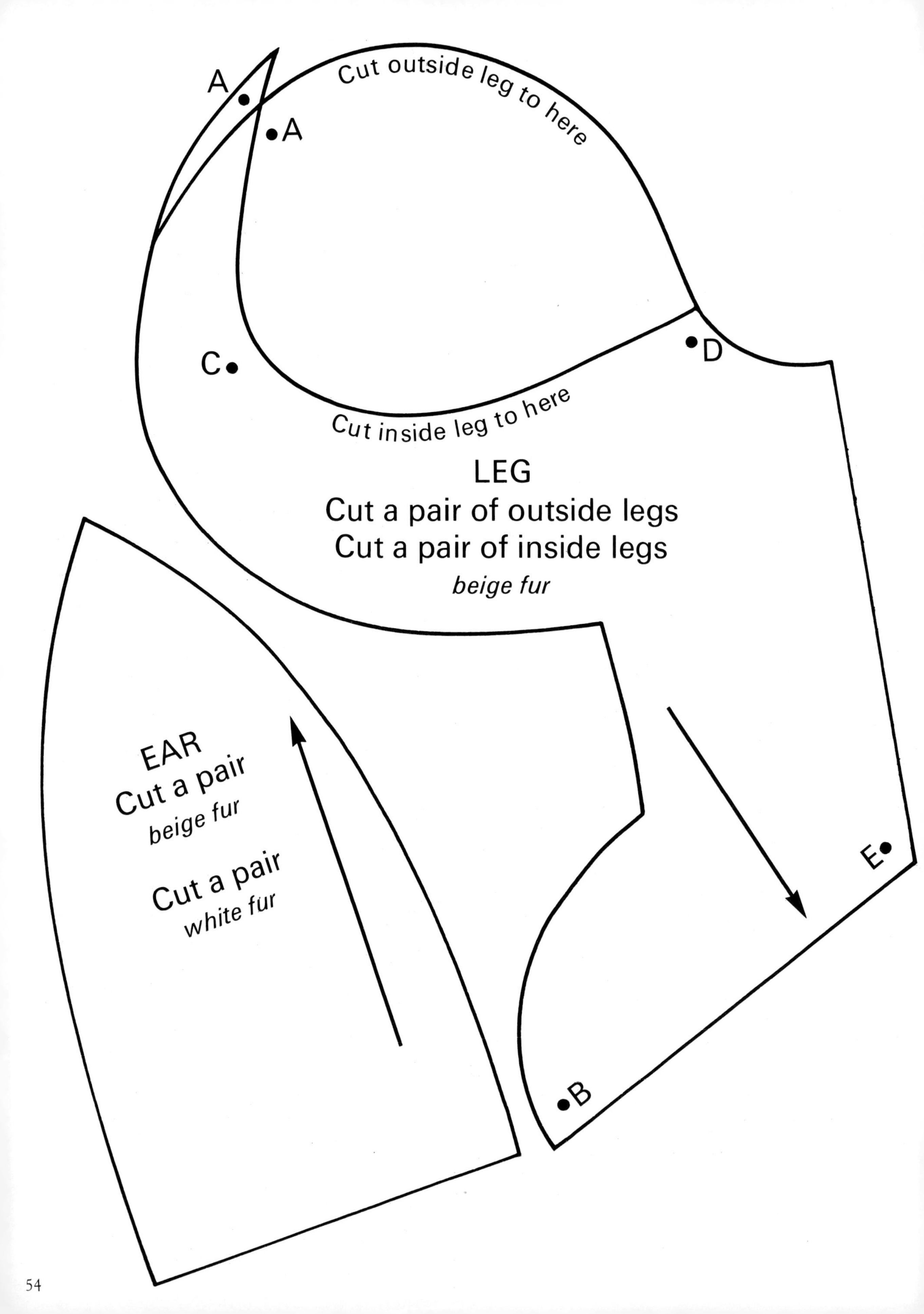
A
A
Cut outside leg to here
C
D
Cut inside leg to here
LEG
Cut a pair of outside legs
Cut a pair of inside legs
beige fur
EAR
Cut a pair
beige fur
Cut a pair
white fur
E
B

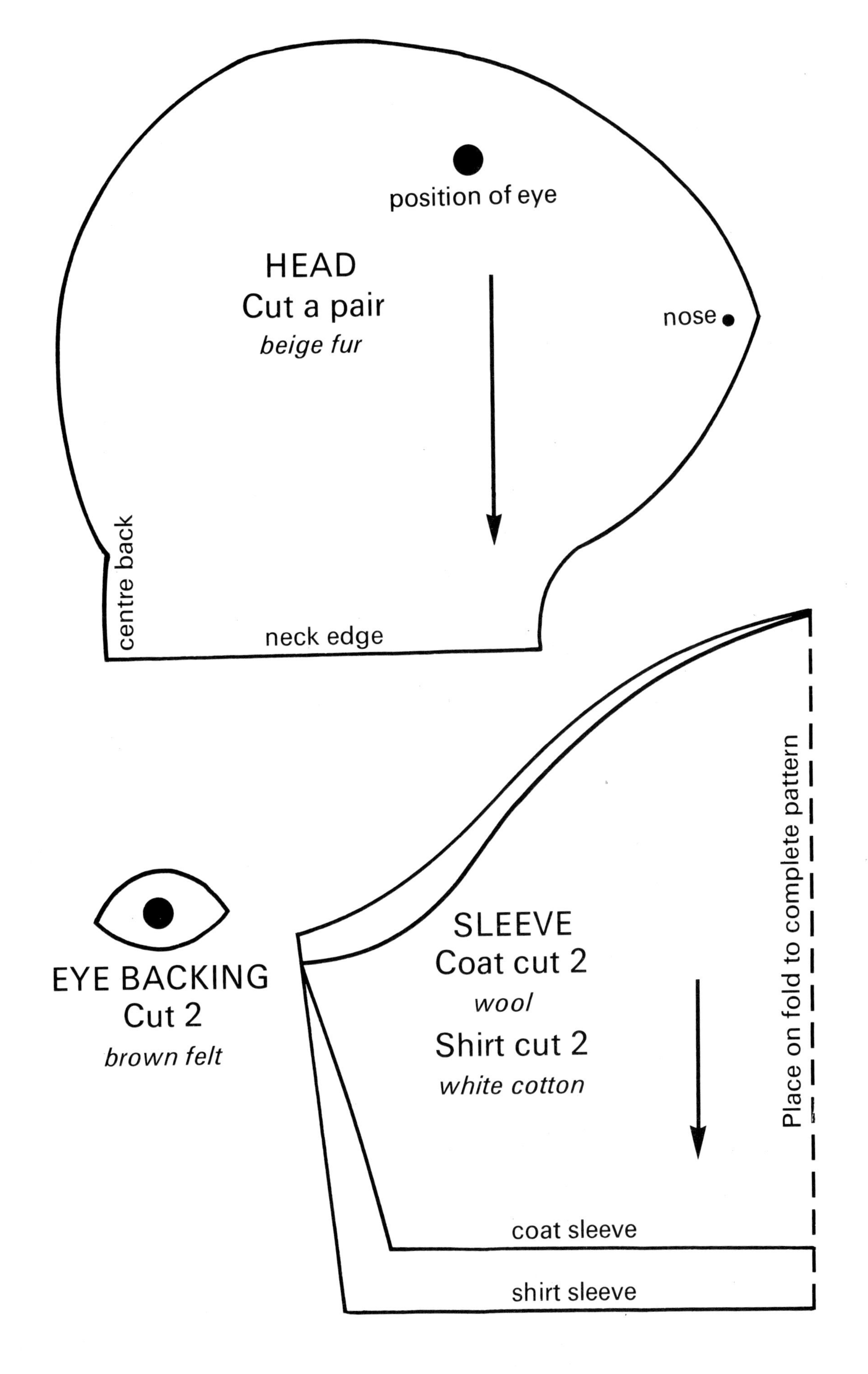
position of eye
HEAD
Cut a pair
beige fur
nose
centre back
neck edge
EYE BACKING
Cut 2
brown felt
SLEEVE
Coat cut 2
wool
Shirt cut 2
white cotton
Place on fold to complete pattern
coat sleeve
shirt sleeve

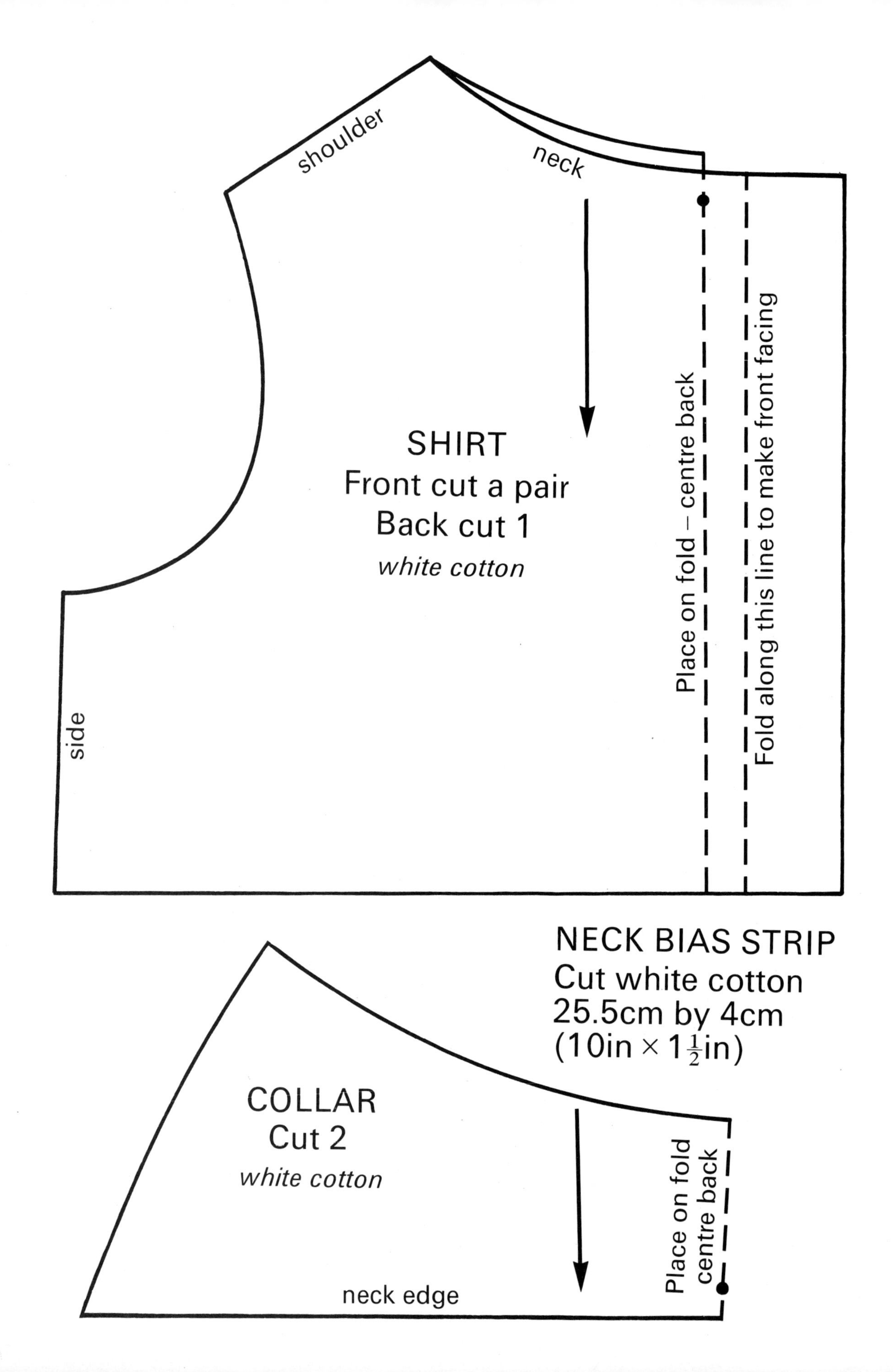
shoulder
neck
SHIRT
Front cut a pair
Back cut 1
white cotton
Place on fold – centre back
Fold along this line to make front facing
side
NECK BIAS STRIP
Cut white cotton
25.5cm by 4cm
(10in × 1½in)
COLLAR
Cut 2
white cotton
Place on fold
centre back
neck edge

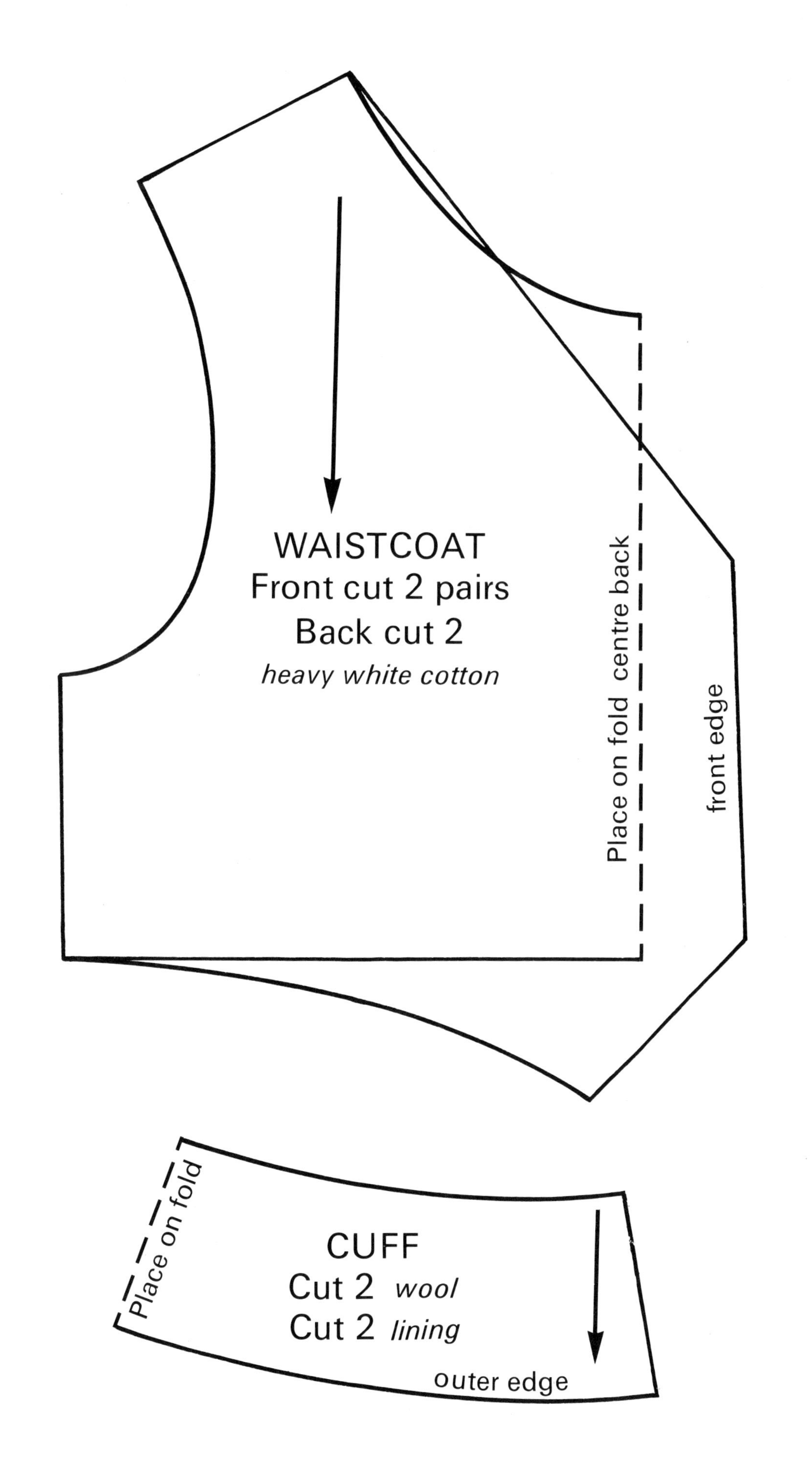
WAISTCOAT
Front cut 2 pairs
Back cut 2
heavy white cotton
Place on fold centre back
front edge
CUFF
Cut 2 *wool*
Cut 2 *lining*
Place on fold
outer edge

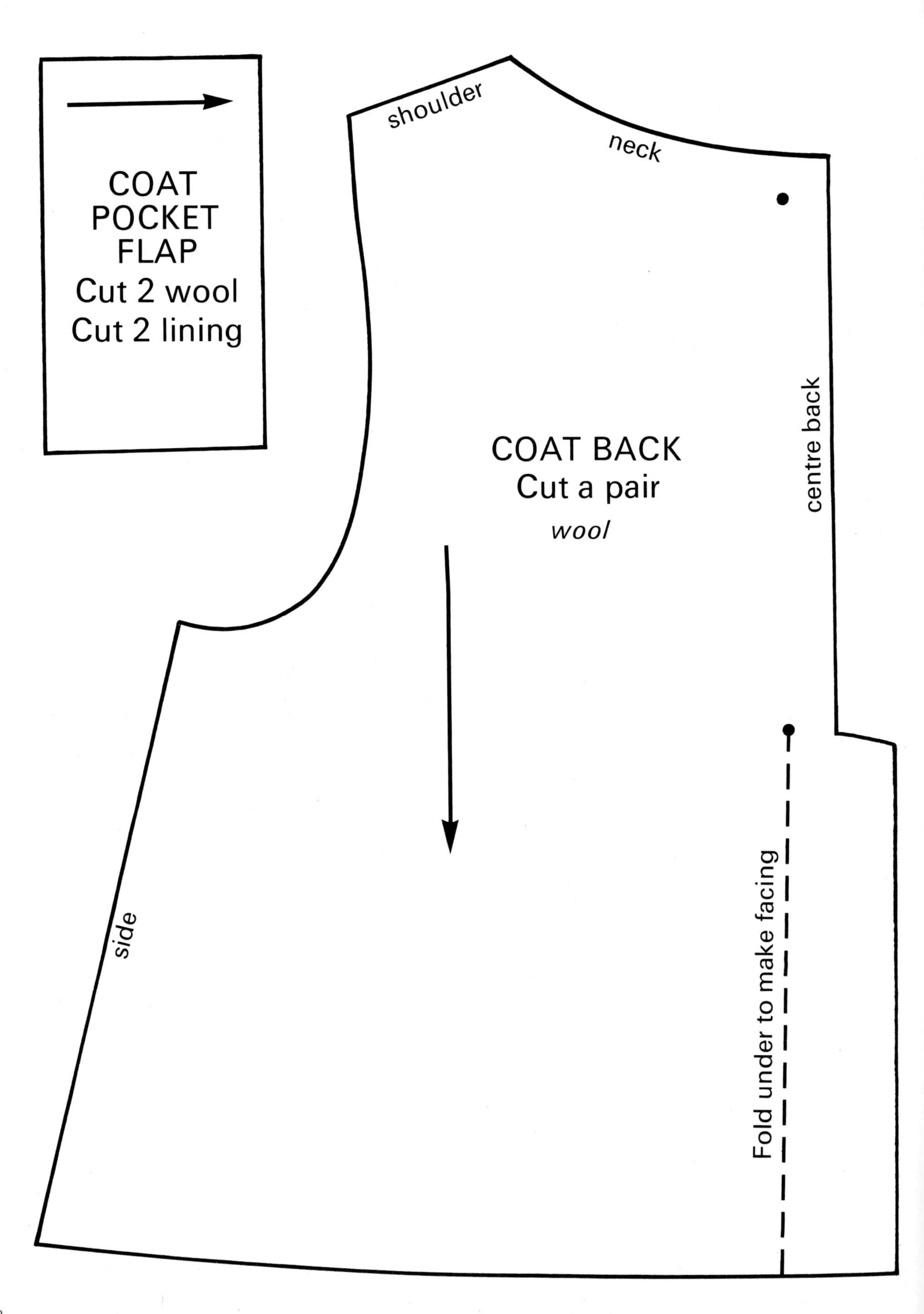
COAT POCKET FLAP
Cut 2 wool
Cut 2 lining
shoulder
neck
COAT BACK
Cut a pair
wool
centre back
side
Fold under to make facing

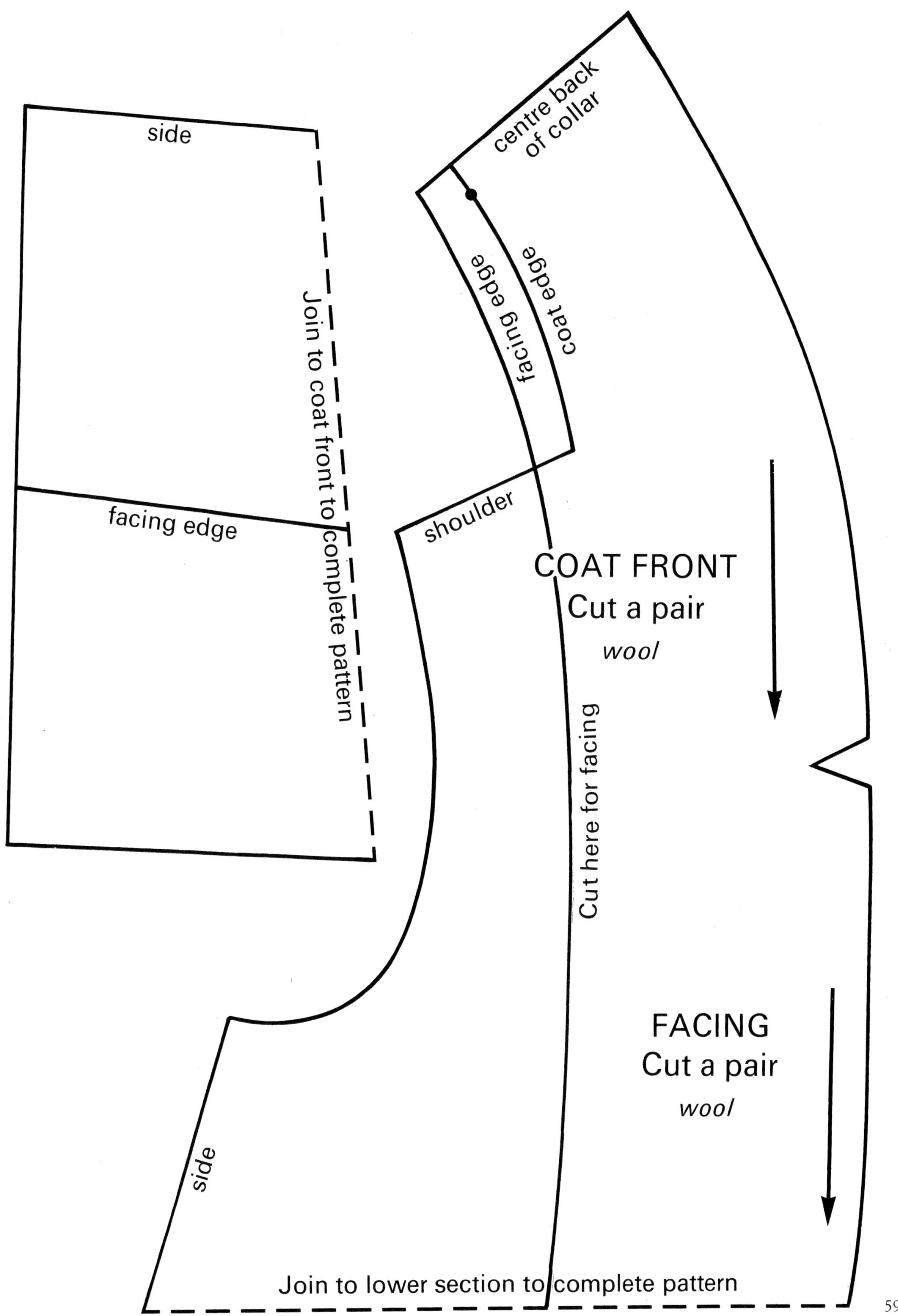
side
Join to coat front to complete pattern
facing edge
centre back of collar
facing edge
coat edge
shoulder
COAT FRONT
Cut a pair
wool
Cut here for facing
FACING
Cut a pair
wool
side
Join to lower section to complete pattern

Making the body

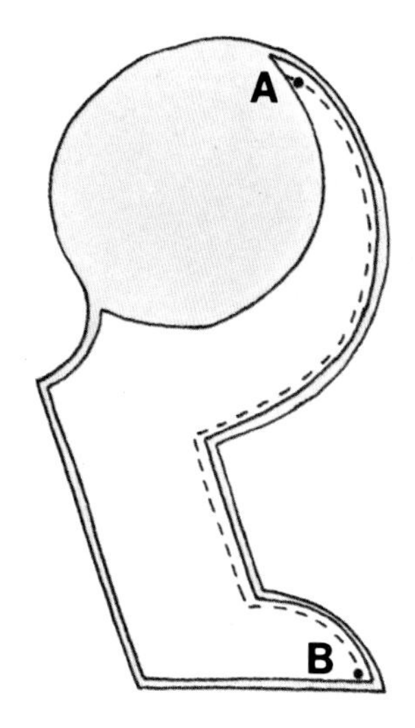

1 Sew a matching inside and outside leg piece together down the front from A to B. Make second leg in the same way but check that you have a pair.

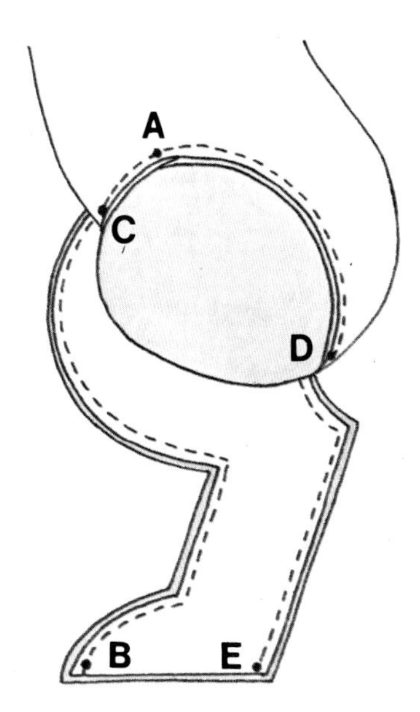

2 Fit top of leg into matching side body and sew inside leg edge to body from C to A and outside leg edge from A to D. The back leg seam from D to E can now be closed. Sew remaining leg to other side body in the same way. Sew a sole to the base of each leg.

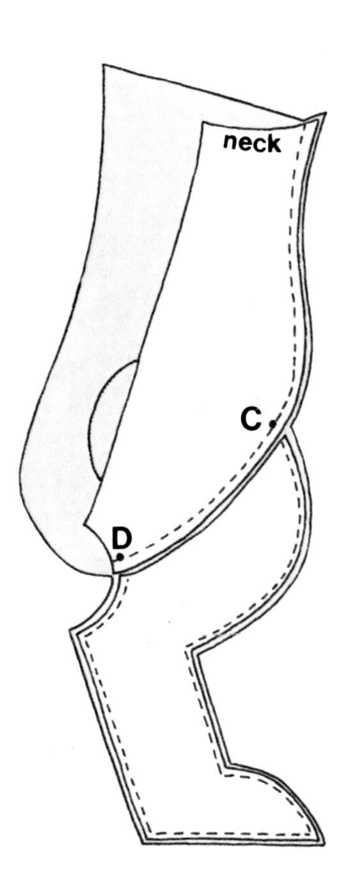

3 Sew front gusset in place from neck edge down through C to D on each front edge of the side bodies in turn.

4 Fit back gusset between back edges of the side bodies and sew from neck edge down to D on both sides in turn. Sew front and back gussets together where they meet between the legs at the two D's.

5 Turn completed body right side out and stuff feet and legs firmly, checking that Hare stands steady. Continue stuffing up to the neck opening, filling out the body into a good rounded, firm shape. Gather up neck edge and fasten off.

6 Sew tail pieces together round the curved shape, tucking in the long pile as you go. Turn tail right side out and bring seams together centrally. Turn in raw edges and sew

edges together. There is no need to stuff the tail as the natural curve of the body will help the tail to hold its shape.

7 Ladder stitch the lower edge of the tail towards the bottom edge of the back gusset. Hold tail close to body by catching inside surface to the gusset as marked on the pattern.

8 Make arms as directed for Little Grey Rabbit (*step 11*) and attach to the body with tape hinges.

9 Sew head pieces together from the nose down to the neck. Fit head gusset between head pieces and sew back from the nose on each side in turn. Finish closing centre back seam of the head down to the neck edge.

10 Turn head right side out and make holes for the eyes. Thread a felt eye backing onto the shank of an eye then fix it in place. Fix second eye in the same way. Stuff the head firmly.

11 Turn under the neck edge shaping the angle at which the head sits on the body. Run a doubled gathering thread around the folded neck edge and pull up. Fasten off gathering and ladder stitch the head to the body.

12 Work nose in same way as described for Little Grey Rabbit (*step 16*) and then sew a fine set of whiskers on each cheek.

13 Sew a white ear lining to a beige ear leaving straight edge open. Pull lining away from the ear and sew an open pleat.

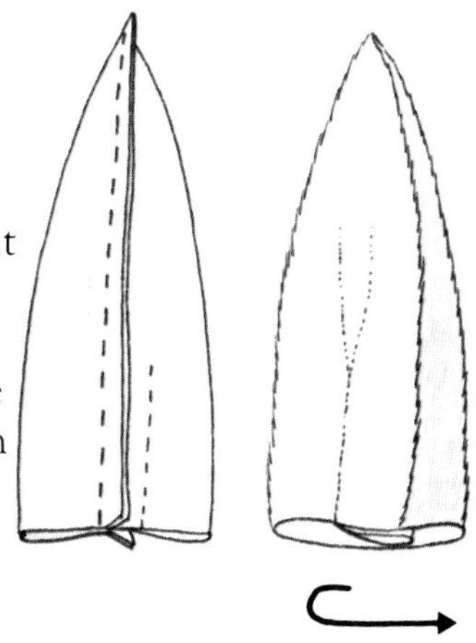

14 Turn ear right side out and finger press pleat to one side. Oversew bottom edges together to hold pleat in place. Make second ear in the same way but fold pleat to the opposite side. Folding the pleat to one side pulls the beige fur forward to frame the inside edge of the ear.

15 Place ears on head with inside edges together on the crown. Ladder stitch in place as described for Little Grey Rabbit (*step 15*).

Now make Hare's clothes

THE SHIRT

1 Fold forward facings on front centre edges and turn under a narrow, single hem. Machine stitch along each fold line and across the top and bottom edges. Now sew fronts to back on the shoulders and press seams open.

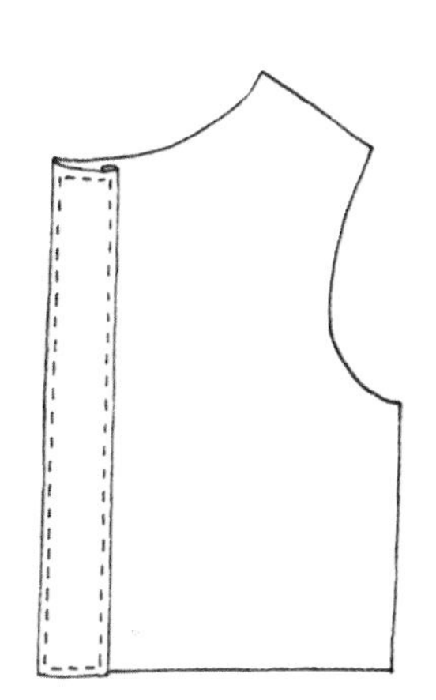

2 Work a row of stay stitching around the neck then clip the edge to open the neck out straight.

3 Sew collars together leaving the neck edge open. Trim seams, clip curves and corners, turn right side out and press. Tack raw edges together.

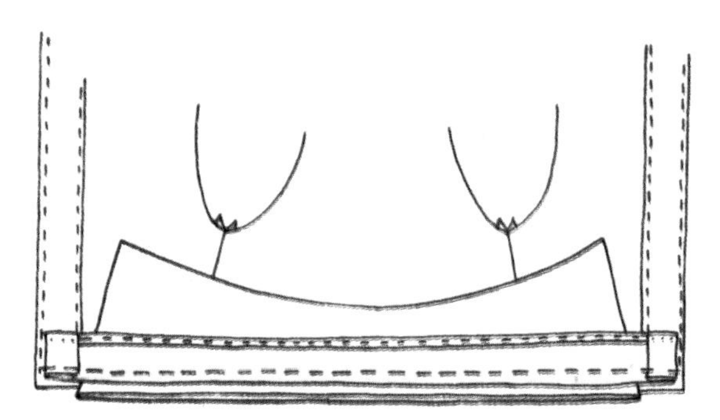

4 Sew collar to shirt with raw edges level, matching the centre backs together and sewing to the front on each side in turn. Neaten one long edge of the neck bias strip then sew raw edge along the neck collar seam with the ends turned forward.

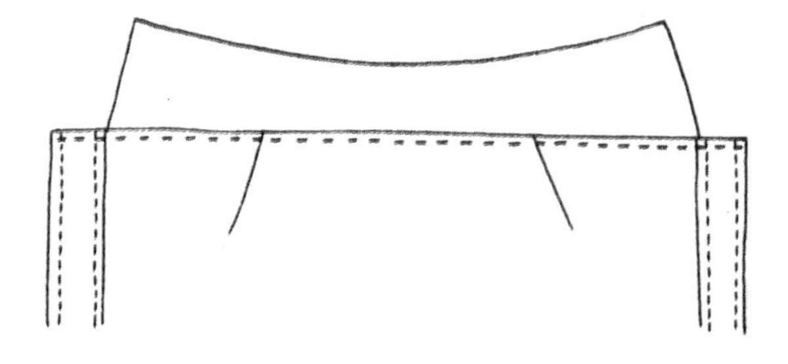

5 Pull collar upwards away from the shirt and turn the bias over to the wrong side. With the right side of the shirt facing upwards, stitch just below the collar seam to hold the bias and shirt together.

6 Fit a sleeve in each armhole and trim seam allowances. Hem wrist edges then close both underarm and side seams.

7 Finish shirt by making a narrow hem along the bottom edge and sewing a press stud at the neck.

THE COAT

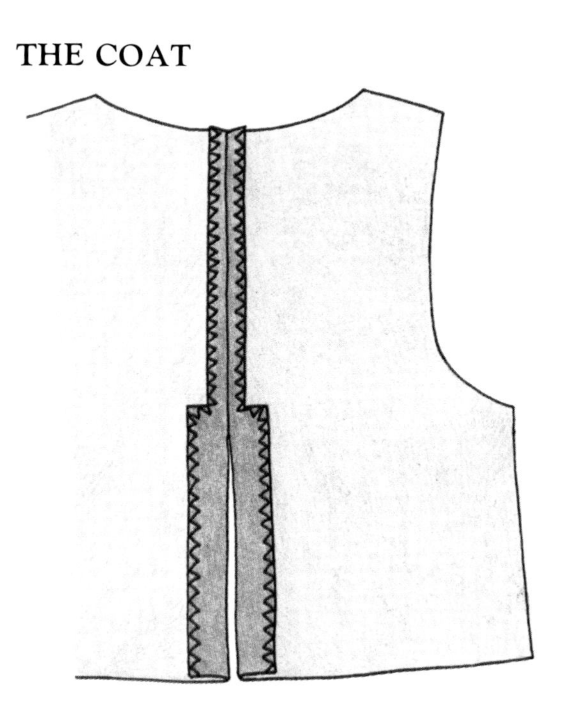

1 Sew backs together down centre back and neaten edges of seam and facing with zigzag stitch. Press both seam and bottom flaps open under a damp cloth. Do not iron back and forth but use a pressing action and block under a weight if possible. This will produce a tailored finish to the coat with very flat seams and sharp creases.

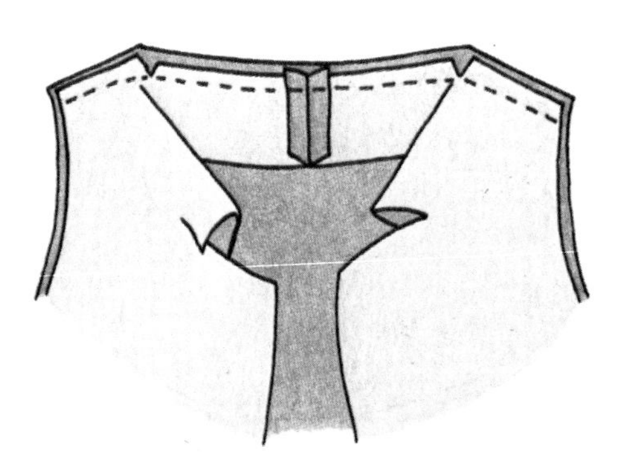

2 Sew coat fronts together at centre back of the collar. Press seam open. Sew fronts to back across the shoulders and back neck edge,

clipping the seam allowance at the corners of the neck so that the collar lies flat. Trim the seam, layer cutting to reduce the bulk.

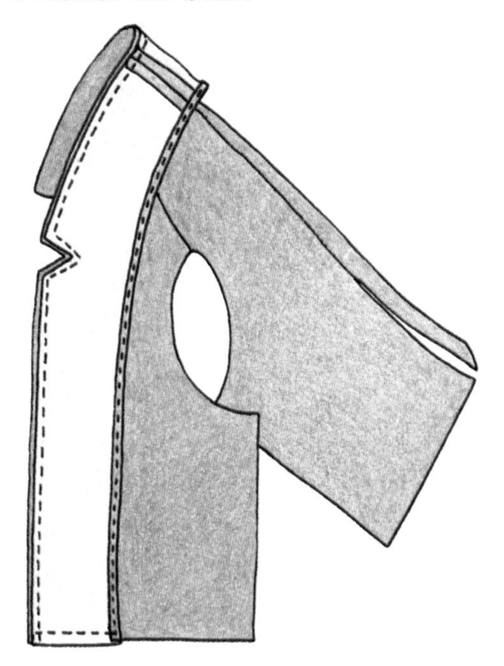

3 Sew front facings together at centre back of the collar and press seam open. Now match facing to coat and sew together from lower front edge up to neck and down to lower edge on the opposite side. Neaten inner edge of facing by sewing a narrow hem. Trim all seams and then sew across the bottom edges to hold facing and coat together. Turn facing right side out, press and block (*see step 1*).

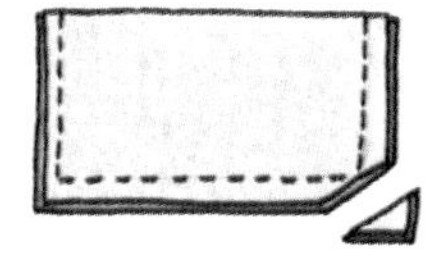

4 Sew a lining to each pocket flap on both short sides and one long edge. Trim seam, turn right side out and press.

5 Place pocket flap on coat front with lining uppermost and flap turned upwards. Sew across, turn flap down

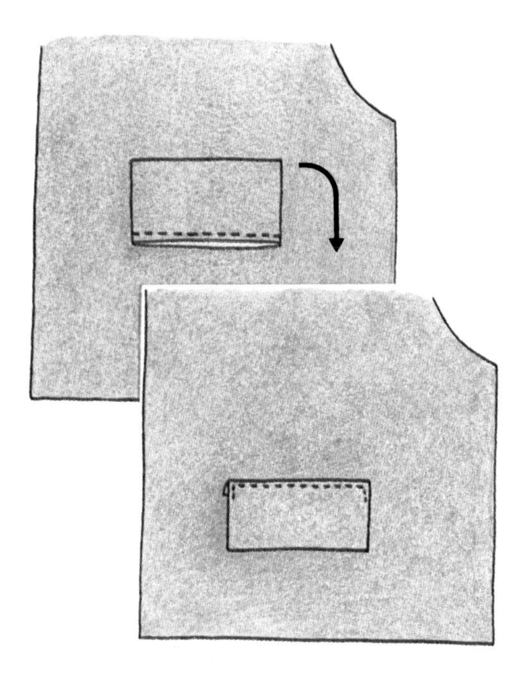

and topstitch across the fold. Complete second pocket flap in the same way.

6 Catch front facing down to coat by sewing them together on the shoulder seams and out of sight behind the two pocket flaps. You can also topstitch the facing to the coat on the neck seam at the centre back. Sew the three buttons on one front side.

7 Prepare sleeves by making the cuffs first. Sew a cotton lining to each cuff along the outer curved edge. Trim seam, turn right sides out and press the seams under a damp cloth. Sew cuff to sleeve with right side of cuff to wrong side of sleeve and all raw edges level. Trim seam and turn cuff to right side of sleeve. Tack sides to sleeve.

8 Fit a sleeve into each armhole, sew and trim the seam allowances. Sew both underarm and side seams. Clip corner at underarm.

9 Turn up lower edge of coat, neaten and hem in place.

THE WAISTCOAT

1 Sew fronts to back at side seams then press side seams open. Make the lining in the same way. Now lay lining and waistcoat right sides together and sew around outside edge as described for Weasel's waistcoat. Trim seams, clip curves, turn right side out and press. Close opening.

2 Sew three press studs on front opening and then four white buttons on the outside. Keep buttons close together.

3 Crochet a length of gold cord for the watch chain. Coil one end of the chain making a disc the size of a small button. Sew disc on waistcoat at waist level where a pocket would be. Sew a small hook on the other end of the chain and work a buttonhole bar on the front of the waistcoat for fastening it.

THE TIE

1 Fold each end of the tie in half and sew the raw edges together. Cut off the folded corners and turn right side out.

2 Press seams flat and shape ends of tie into points. A few catch stitches will hold the facings down. Dress tie on Hare folding at the back of the neck to reduce the width. Tuck ends inside the waistcoat.

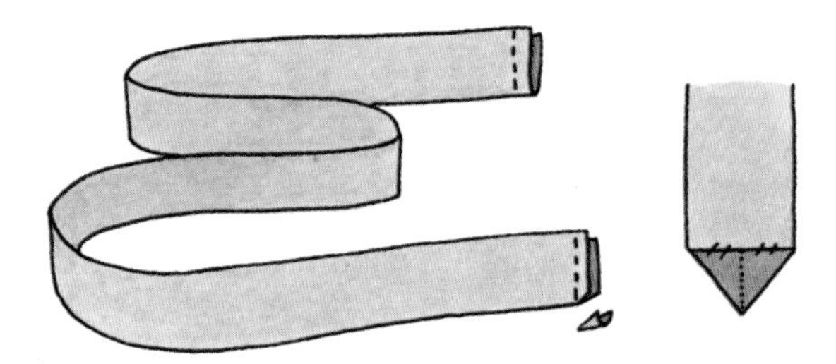